P O E The Detective

Other Books by JOHN WALSH

The Shroud

Strange Harp, Strange Symphony

POE THE DETECTIVE

The Curious Circumstances Behind

The Mystery of Marie Roget

JOHN WALSH

Rutgers University Press

New Brunswick, New Jersey

Dedicated to my sister

PATRICIA KELLY

who loves a mystery

Preface

This book has taken some dozen years to grow from a seed of idle curiosity planted by Edgar Allan Poe's bold claim that he had solved a real-life murder mystery without leaving the comfort of his arm-chair. Since my first determination to test that claim, I have pursued the subject irregularly, and it was not till I was fairly sure I had traced all the lines and rounded all the corners that I ventured to set down the results. Others before me, with more or less diligence, have interested themselves in the topic, but they have all come away with a somewhat hazy notion that the irritable genius of American letters may indeed have done what he said he did. In these pages, I feel, the chase finally comes to an end, and I can only express my thanks to the talented, if slippery, Mr. Poe for making it such a merry one. Despite the conclusions reached herein, I think he would be pleased to find that one of the least considered of his writings can still cause such a fuss.

J. W.

New York, April 1967

Contents

List of Illustrations

P O E The Detective

There is yet a mystery
in this business which time
alone can unravel.

> New York *Herald*
>
> August 23, 1841

Introduction by Thomas Ollive Mabbott

This is a detective story about a detective story. It reads like a well-written work of fiction, but the scholarship is sound, and the amount of research it has involved is far more than might be apparent to a reader who has not worked in the dusty files of the newspapers of the second quarter of the last century. Dusty they are indeed, but not crumbling, for rag paper was still used—and although the type was small, they were well printed.

The detective studied is of course Monsieur C. Auguste Dupin, whose alter ego is Edgar Allan Poe. His spiritual ancestor was Voltaire's Zadig, and he probably descends from one of the Princes of Serendip whose adventures were given to the world at least as long ago as 1557. But it was Poe who gave us the literary genre—for no detective story since his day is without trace of his direct or indirect influence. "The Murders in the Rue Morgue" was the first detective story deliberately composed as such. Poe gave us the models. He discovered the genus and all the important species. Even the kind in which the criminal is disguised by his respectability was presented in "Thou Art the Man."

The second of Poe's detective stories is the first to be wholly "founded on fact," for Dupin attempted to solve a real mystery— the death of a New York cigar girl, Mary Cecilia Rogers.

That Mary was beautiful goes without saying. John Anderson imported from London the custom of having pretty girls sell tobacco, but his first girl was Mary, an American whose charms

attracted numerous leading citizens, including editors, to the store.
No wonder her mysterious death had such a sensational news value
in a day when the elder James Gordon Bennett had begun to print
all the news, without caring if it was fit to print.

Poe had a keen sense of what would interest his public. He read
"many a quaint and curious volume of forgotten lore" with an eye
for what might prove useful to a writer of stories, and he satirized
his own method in his grotesque comic tale "How to Write a
Blackwood Article." But he also read current books and periodicals
—especially newspapers—looking for "his own where he found it."
His originality lay in the skilful combination of incidents and ideas
which he said he "selected or invented," and like the greatest English
and French playwrights, he selected far more than he made up.

The selections were as varied as Poe's tales, but all journalists have
an interest in crime. Poe was, despite his known preference for a
poetical career, for practical reasons a magazinist. The story called
"Diddling Considered as One of the Exact Sciences" is a collection
of petty rogueries. Although nobody has yet pointed out all of Poe's
sources, the trick of a rogue who posed as a toll gatherer when a
large crowd was expected to cross a toll-free bridge was played
near Wheeling (now in West Virginia) according to the New York
Rover of September 14, 1844.

The "monkey criminal" of "The Murders in the Rue Morgue" had
a predecessor in real life—a baboon who was thought to be trained
to climb in windows to steal, of whom there is a rather detailed
account in the *Shrewsbury Chronicle,* published at Ipswich, England,
August 22, 1834—which gave rise to articles Poe presumably had seen.

"The Oblong Box" (not a story of crime as Poe told it) is based in
part on the murder of the printer Samuel Adams by John C. Colt—
which succeeded the death of Mary Rogers as the leading sensational
topic for the American press.

In those stories—and others could be cited—there was a good deal
of material from other sources than what Poe read in the papers. In
"The Mystery of Marie Roget" the newspapers were professedly his
only sources; and in the second printing of his tale Poe even named
those he quoted and followed. He did follow them, although through
Dupin's eyes he saw that some were unreliable, and said so, and
analyzed what he accepted.

Poe used only the newspapers he had before him, and used them well for the most part. What Poe used badly was the remark of Mrs. Rogers that she would "never see Mary again." Dupin did not see more than a hint that the old lady had some idea that her daughter planned to elope.

What follows is Mr. Walsh's story. He has drawn on original sources, especially the newspaper files of 1841 and 1842. His researches were practically completed when I met him and showed him the material assembled for annotation of the Belknap Press *Complete Works* of Poe. He knew some things that I did not, and needed little but verifications of two or three dates of papers preserved only in libraries outside of New York City. It may be added that I am in complete agreement with Mr. Walsh that the whole account of the lost boat found adrift (which is not essential to Poe's proposed solution) is the author's invention. For safety from libel suits Poe had to be ready to prove his story was fiction. Mr. Walsh's detective story has no element of fiction at all, but is no less absorbing for that reason.

CHAPTER ONE

Hark! heard ye not that note of fear
Burst wildly on the palsied ear,
   Far in the tangled wood?

        "Lines on the death of M.R.,"
   by E. S., New York *Herald*, September 27, 1841

Murder in Old New York

O F THE five dozen tales, burlesques and *bizarreries* written by
Edgar Allan Poe, none has had a more curious existence
than *The Mystery of Marie Roget*, the novelette in which
he tried to solve a real-life murder using only newspaper
accounts of the case. Its special distinction arises not from the mere
attempt, nor from the fact that it is one of the three stories in which
Poe founded modern detective fiction,[1] but from the circumstance
that he claimed positively to have succeeded. Because of that claim
an appreciable body of literature—respectable in bulk, if not always
in quality—has grown up around the story. Some of it argues that
Poe did solve the case, some that he didn't, and some of it even
continues to offer solutions to the murder itself. One comparatively
recent treatment suggests the possibility of Poe being the murderer,[2]
an idea which serves as a fair example of the lengths to which *Marie
Roget* has driven those who would pry into her secret.

    Poe's biographers avoid serious discussion of the story, classing it,
from the viewpoint of art, among his less successful writings, and the
least interesting of the three Dupin tales. They make scant and
usually erroneous reference to its factual basis—the mysterious death

of a young New York girl, Mary Rogers, whose body was found in the Hudson River in July, 1841. One of the most complete and popular biographies, for instance, Hervey Allen's *Israfel,* gives *The Mystery of Marie Roget* no more than a 13-line footnote which concludes rather archly: "This is *all* enormously characteristic of the time and the man."[3] A more recent popularization, Frances Winwar's *The Haunted Palace,* contains so many errors regarding the real case that it becomes a perplexing task merely to decide what her sources were. Still, she manages to leave with the reader the impression that Poe did solve the mystery![4] Even the careful work published by Arthur Hobson Quinn in 1941 shows a surprisingly weak grasp of the story and its factual background—or shows, to be precise, a notable blindness in the face of clear evidence. Quinn asserts that Poe didn't claim to solve the Mary Rogers mystery, but merely used it as an example of how such a case should be handled by the police. As proof he offers a sentence from a letter in which Poe describes his object as the "analysis of the *principles of investigation* in cases of like character."[5] But Quinn chose from the letter what suited him, and a somewhat different impression is gained if the preceding portion of the same letter is highlighted:

> Under pretense of showing how Dupin (the hero of the Rue Morgue) unravelled the mystery of Marie's assassination, I, in fact, enter into a very rigorous analysis of the real tragedy in New York. *No point* is omitted. I examine, each by each, the opinions and arguments of our press on the subject, and show (I think satisfactorily) that this subject has never yet been *approached.* The press has been entirely on the wrong scent. In fact, I really believe, not only that I have demonstrated the falsity of the idea that the girl was the victim of a gang, but have *indicated the assassin . . . .*[6]

Poe's final statement in the matter, which was footnoted to the reprint of the story in the 1845 volume of *Tales,* and which has clung tenaciously to it ever since, is sufficiently convincing: "All argument founded upon the fiction is applicable to the truth: and the investigation of the truth was the object." Professor Quinn, a model of scholarly sincerity, has merely been caught in one of the volatile Poe's double shuffles.

It is hardly surprising, after all this, to find that in an otherwise careful, full-scale study of the history of detective fiction, the uncertainty about *Marie Roget* is continued. A. E. Murch, while briefly discussing *Marie Roget,* explains that "Dupin gave a practical demonstration of his detective powers by putting forward an explanation of a mystery that had aroused the excited interest of the American public for several months before this tale appeared . . . a case that was still unsolved when Poe's story was published." Having thus prepared the reader, Murch descends to the comparative safety of a footnote to complete the commentary: "When, a few years later, this story was issued with others in volume form, notes were added to explain the circumstances under which it was written, and to point out that Dupin's deductions proved correct in every detail."[7] Murch, however, was not sufficiently concerned to delve any deeper, and readers are left to draw their own conclusions.

Interestingly enough, Poe's first real biographer, John Ingram, found it necessary in 1880, only thirty years after his subject's death, to remind his readers that *Marie Roget* was not solely a product of the imagination: "Latterly it has been the fashion (especially among foreigners) to disbelieve that *Marie Roget*'s mystery had any real existence, and that the whole recital was but the coinage of the poet's brain. . . . Nevertheless, such was not the case; the narrative was founded on fact, although the incidents of the tragedy differed widely from those recounted in the tale." Despite Ingram, however, there was never much doubt that the story was entirely based on solid fact, differing in no important aspect from the real event. The whole sad tale still lives in the closely printed columns of the old New York newspapers: for the month of August, and parts of September and October, 1841, an avid public was served up almost daily reports of the police investigation, along with liberal portions of guesses, theories and extraneous information.

The murdered girl, Mary Cecilia Rogers, was not a public figure, and subsequent writers have usually had to wrench the truth a little to explain why her tragic fate rated so much attention. Death by violence, whether accidental or not, was a rather common, and very often bizarre, occurrence in the New York of the early eighteen-hundreds. The Hudson River frequently gave up the body of some man or woman who had found a grave in it, and more than once corpses were found packed and labeled like regular cargo on New

York's piers, destined for illegal dissecting rooms.[8] Such happenings
were usually given one or two paragraphs and no follow-up,
journalism not yet having learned, or at least not yet having
surrendered to, the circulation value of sensationalism. To account
for Mary's posthumous leap to such unwonted prominence, most
writers have recognized the need for some reason besides the girl's
violent death, so they have conveniently endowed her with varying
degrees of fame or at least notoriety. Her position as a countergirl in
a tobacco store, as well as supposedly exceptional beauty of face and
figure—the papers promptly labeled her "The Beautiful Cigar
Girl"—are given as reasons why she had been "adored and respected
by customers of consequence," or had been so well known that her
death caused "amazement and consternation." In a city with a
population in 1840 of just over 300,000, and where the majority of
the inhabitants were concentrated within a few square miles at the
lower end of Manhattan, some local fame for an otherwise obscure
young beauty would not have been impossible, but the real reason
for the intense public interest in her fate was less connected with
personal fame than with the times in which she lived.

She was, it is clear, among the first to gain celebrity as a by-
product of journalism's dawning self-consciousness. Within a week
of her death, the New York *Daily Express* gave the story a front-
page headline, explaining that the murder was of "such an atrocious
character as to demand that it be taken forth from the ordinary
police reports, to be made a matter of especial attention, in order if
possible, to arouse inquiry as to the murderers."[9] Four days after
that, the New York *Atlas* defended the interest of the city's papers
in the case: "Who caused any stir to be made to discover the
murderers of Mary C. Rogers? The Press!"[10] Mary's house,
moreover, at 126 Nassau Street, was located in the very heart of
New York's newspaper industry—the offices of more than twenty
papers and periodicals were situated on Nassau Street alone, within
a few seconds' walk of her house, and as many more were scattered
through the surrounding streets. Horace Greeley's New York
Tribune and James Gordon Bennett's New York *Herald* were both
just around the corner on Ann Street; murder on the doorstep,
whether of a cat or a king, can scarcely be overlooked.

Little is known about Mary before the tragedy. She had been

Contemporary sketch
of Mary Rogers behind the counter
at Anderson's cigar store

born about 1820, presumably in New York (though one paper gave
her a Connecticut origin[11]), the child of Daniel and Phoebe Rogers.
City directories, even for those early days, listed thousands of names
but Daniel Rogers does not appear in any of them. A nationwide
financial crisis occurred in 1837, and it was probably this event that
led Mary to look for work when she was only seventeen; her father
had died some years before in a steamboat explosion on the
Mississippi.[12] She found a position with John Anderson, a twenty-
five-year-old tobacco merchant, who hired her to work behind the
counter in his store on upper Broadway.[13]

The use of young girls as attractions in establishments where the
trade was predominantly male was a new departure for the times.
(The ease with which such arrangements are accepted today

beclouds the misgivings of our ancestors on the subject; in the
eighteen-forties female employment in such places was considered a
daring and dangerous exposure of innocence to the corruption of
the world.) From what is known about Mary, she must have fitted
in with the practice admirably. If she was not the sultry beauty that
later writers have imagined, she was at least pretty, with a wealth of
shining black hair and a "dark smile." One close acquaintance
described her as "amiable and pleasing, and rather fascinating in her
manners," and most of the news accounts depict her in such or
similar terms. In a store where the trade was almost entirely male,
the sight of Mary flouncing behind the neat rows of snuff and
tobacco must have caused more than one man to come back a second
time. Some verses that appeared in the *Herald* soon after her death
indicate that she did, indeed, have the desired impact on the
neighborhood's smokers:

She moved amid the bland perfume
That breathes of heaven's balmiest isle;
Her eyes had starlight's azure gloom
And a glimpse of heaven—her smile

. . . .

Who that has loitered up Broadway
But marked her mid the evening light,
(Encircled by the young and gay)
With face that said her soul was right![14]

If later accounts describing Anderson's clientele are true (and
there is some contemporary mention), Mary had a stimulating time
in her work. The store is reputed to have been the favorite lounging
place for the city's reporters and editors, as well as a crowd of
Broadway gamblers—a curious parlay. Some famous names are also
connected with the store: James Fenimore Cooper, at the height of
his fame, and Washington Irving, who had his *Adventures of
Captain Bonneville* in the press in 1837, may both have been
regular customers. Fitz-Green Halleck, then regarded as a poet of
high rank, is said to have written some lines to Mary, but if so they
were never published.[15] By some it is claimed that Poe himself
frequented the store and was acquainted with Mary; they urge that
in any case it would be entirely natural for Poe to use the same

tobacconist favored by his journalistic brethren. This may well be, but the tradition can be traced back no earlier than 1887 when it appeared, without documentation, in George Walling's *Recollections of a New York Police Chief*. Since then, because it lends a decidedly nice touch to the whole affair, commentators have tended to quote it as at least probable, some going so far as to make Poe and Mary good friends.

It is true that when Mary worked at Anderson's, Poe lived in New York, first on Sixth Avenue and later on Carmine Street, both about fifteen minutes' walk or five minutes' ride from the store. And it is also true that he mixed, or tried to mix, in journalism circles: he had come to New York from Richmond, after losing his position as editor of the *Southern Literary Messenger,* with the hope of reestablishing himself in magazine work. But, while it is probable that in his strolls on Broadway he may more than once have passed Anderson's store while Mary was holding court inside, known fact cannot place him any nearer than ten blocks away, about a half mile. William Gowans, an acquaintance of Poe's, kept a bookstore at 169 Broadway, and here Poe supposedly was a frequent visitor.[16] No one today, however, can say more than that he *might* have bought cigars from Mary Rogers, and it should be understood that whether he did or did not, the point has no great relevance. By the summer of 1838 he had left the city for Philadelphia, still seeking a livelihood.

The understandable fears that Mary's mother felt about letting her daughter spend her days in a world of men all too quickly took on disconcerting shape. In 1838—two years and eight months before her death—something happened involving Mary which even today, after all the research, still isn't clear. On Thursday, October 5th, 1838, four morning papers carried brief items to the effect that a certain Mary Cecilia Rogers had disappeared from her home, then located on Pitt Street, and had left behind a note saying that she was going to kill herself. Since this little episode becomes a crucial element in Poe's story, these paragraphs are of some importance. From the New York *Sun:*

> *Something mysterious*—A Mrs. Hays [Mary's aunt] yesterday evening brought to the coroner a letter which Miss Mary Cecilia Rogers, a young lady who recently attended Anderson's cigar store in Broadway, adjoining

the hospital-yard, had yesterday left at the house of her mother, No. 114 Pitt Street, which letter informed her mother that she had left home forever, for the purpose of putting an end to her life, and bidding her mother an affectionate and final farewell. Alarmed by the appalling announcement, the terrified mother caused search to be made for her daughter in every place where she thought it possible she could have resorted either for the fulfillment of her dreadful purpose or for concealment; but no trace of her could be discovered up to yesterday morning. She is twenty years of age and when she left home she was dressed in a brown satin frock, Tuscan hat, and had a small red handkerchief round her neck. Any information which will throw any light on what has become of her, will be gratefully received by her afflicted mother at the above place. The cause of this wayward freak of the young lady, is supposed by her friends to be disappointed love—she having recently received the addresses of a certain widower, who it is said, has deserted her and by his desertion has brought upon her a state of mind which has prompted her, it is feared, to commit self-destruction.

The facts given by the New York *Journal of Commerce* were nearly identical, even to the dress, the hat and the handkerchief:

CORONER'S OFFICE.—Supposed Love and Suicide.—An elderly lady called yesterday evening at the Coroner's office and showed his clerk a letter which had been that morning found on the dressing table of a young lady who had a few hours before left home, since which no trace could be found of her, and her friends feared that she had committed suicide. The letter was written by a Miss Mary Cecilia Rogers, who resided at 114 Pitt Street, and was directed to her mother. In this letter the young lady took an affectionate farewell of her mother, and informed her that she had left home with the fixed and unalterable determination to destroy herself. As soon as the mother of the young lady received the letter, she sent messengers in different directions in search of her daughter, but up to a late hour yesterday evening they had not succeeded in discovering any trace of her. The young lady, it appears, had some time back attended in a store in Broadway, and while there had been for several months paid particular attention by a gentleman, who since ceased his attentions and left the city, and it is supposed that this occurrence has so operated on the young lady's mind as to produce the occurrence we relate. When leaving her mother's house yesterday morning, she was dressed in a brown satin frock, Tuscan hat, and wore a small red silk handkerchief on her neck.[17]

The New York *Times and Commercial Intelligencer* reiterated the basic story and added some incidental details, in a tone so flippant as to be entirely out of keeping with even the primitive journalism of the time:

Love and Supposed Suicide.—Mrs. Hays of No. 114 Pitt Street, applied
yesterday afternoon at the Coroner's Office for advice how to act in the
following case. The lady stated that a girl named Mary Cecilia Rogers, had
suddenly left her residence that morning, leaving a letter addressed to her
mother, in which she said she could never return again, and concluded by
begging her brother to take care of his aged parent. It seems that Miss
Rogers was employed in Anderson's segar store in Broadway. There she
met and fell in love with a gallant gay Lothario, whose name did not
transpire. After a month's course of billing and cooing across the counter
of Anderson's store, which ended like the smoke of one of that gentleman's
segars (not however to speak disparagingly of their departed worth) in
thin air. The Lothario was one morning found missing and that is the
reason why Miss Rogers is now missing.

When she left she took with her a shilling, as it is supposed, with the
intention of purchasing poison. Her dress was a brown satin frock, Tuscan
hat, and a small red handkerchief round her neck. We are requested to
state that information will be gratefully received at the residence of her
mother, 114 Pitt Street.

It was all sufficiently exciting, but the very next day the whole
affair was denied in the *Times and Commercial Intelligencer:*

A Correspondent who says he is well acquainted with the parties in the
"Love and Suicide" affair published yesterday, gives a quite different
version of it and states that the story is without the least foundation—got
up by some evil-disposed person, who addressed a letter to the mother
amounting in substance to that published yesterday. Miss R. only went on
a visit to a friend in Brooklyn. She is now at home with her mother.[18]

A week later, on October 13th, 1838, the New York *Weekly
Herald* commented editorially: "The recent affair of the young girl
in Anderson's cigar store must lead every reflecting person and every
good member of the community to desire that something should be
done instantly to remedy the great evil consequent upon very
beautiful young girls being placed in cigar and confectionary stores.
. . . Designing rich rascals drop into these places, buy cigars and
sugar plums, gossip with the girl and ultimately affect her ruin . . .
young girls should attend only in those stores where the customers
are ladies." With that admonition the subject was dropped and
Mary faded back into obscurity. But after her death in 1841 some
people would "remember" things about this curious interlude that
had never reached the papers at the time. The *Herald,* on August 3d,
1841, stated: "This young girl, Mary Rogers, was missing from

Anderson's store three years ago for two weeks. It is asserted that she was then seduced by an officer of the U.S. Navy and kept at Hoboken for two weeks. His name is well known on board his ship." The New York *Commercial Advertiser,* on August 25th, 1841, contributed the information that Mary in 1838 had been "abducted or allowed herself to be abducted," or had gone "into concealment that it might be believed she had been abducted, in order to . . . help the sale of the goods of her employer." Another paper admitted that such a story had been circulated at the time, but that, far from its being true, Mary became so angry when she heard it that she quit her job at Anderson's.[19]

The intersection of Broadway and Ann Street, in New York City, at the southern tip of City Hall Park. To the right are the Astor House Hotel and St. Paul's Church, with Trinity Church in the distance. Nassau Street, and Mary Rogers' house at No. 126, was one block down Ann Street, to the left.

Thus two distinctly different answers to the 1838 disappearance were offered by those who professed inside knowledge of the affair: a seduction or a publicity stunt. But there is a third possibility which, to one who has been immersed in the world of the eighteen-forties, is much the more probable. The New York *Sunday News,* on August 10, 1841, with imprecise memory, but with the air of one who possessed privileged information, stated that "many of the reporters for the public press frequented this store, and one undertook to practice a cruel and unjustifiable hoax." This was ratified by the New York weekly, *Brother Jonathan,* which claimed that: "Some penny-a-liner trumped up a tale that she had eloped."[20] In the same connection, it is worthy of remark that the denial of the "Love and Suicide" story on October 6th appeared in the same paper—*The Times and Commercial Intelligencer*—that had carried the "gallant gay Lothario" account, with its surprising tone of levity. Mary was certainly involved with at least one reporter, a young man named Canter: shortly after her death, the *Herald* revealed that Canter, who worked for the *Journal of Commerce,* "was severely beaten about a year ago, by three or four rivals, in consequence of visiting her."[21]

Anyone accustomed to present-day, high-powered journalism cannot easily understand the atmosphere that could give rise to such a "hoax," but early American newspapers were incredibly rife with such playfulness. A particularly glaring example of the grotesque sense of humor that lay back of newspaper hoaxes is a story that appeared in the *Atlas* during the very days of the first excitement over Mary's death. In morbid detail the *Atlas* told its horrified readers that a Mr. Brown of Greenwich Street had risen from his bed in the early hours one morning and methodically clubbed his wife and three children to death. At the end of the gruesome account it was implied that Mr. Brown was insane because he repeatedly mumbled something about protecting his family from mosquitoes. A couple of days later the paper was gleefully telling its readers that the story was a hoax, and a successful one, which is what counted. Dozens of people, it claimed, had been taken in and had actually visited Greenwich Street to observe the site of the atrocities. The paper admitted that some people condemned it for the trick, but they were only the bad sports who had been fooled; anyone who had guessed the little game had pronounced it "capital!"[22] This sort of thing was so prevalent that the public had developed a habitual skepticism for protection, and almost nothing was believed solely on the strength of its appearance in print.

How long Mary continued at Anderson's after the flurry of excitement is not certain. In any case, she did not work there beyond mid-1839, at which time a brother of hers, freshly enriched from some business venture, is supposed to have given Mrs. Rogers enough money to open a boardinghouse. This brother is heard of no more; he preceded his sister to a watery death in the Hudson, being accidentally knocked overboard from his ship as it was outward bound late in 1840.[23]

The house Mrs. Rogers rented stood at No. 126 Nassau Street, around the corner from the famous Park Theater and only a minute's walk from City Hall. It was a narrow brick building, probably of three floors, no different from the others that lined the cobblestoned street, but it gave Mary and her mother a comfortable living. Here for the next two years the girl existed in dutiful obscurity, safe from the "designing rich rascals" who hovered about Anderson's store. During this time the house seems to have been fairly full: the U.S. Census records for 1840, for instance, list a "Pheeby Rogers," New York, Ward 2, as head of a household that included four males, five females and a child.[24] Of these boarders, only the names of William Kiekuck,[25] Alfred Crommeline, Archibald Padley and Daniel Payne have survived. All four would find themselves involved in Mary's fate.

July 25th in 1841 was a Sunday. The sun rose early and quickly threw a pall of suffocating heat over New York City, the temperature eventually reaching 93 degrees. At ten o'clock Mary left her room on the second floor, went down the stairs and stopped at the door of Daniel Payne. According to Payne, she interrupted his shaving to tell him she was going uptown to her aunt's house in Jane Street (a Mrs. Downing) to take her nephews and nieces to church. Payne agreed to meet her at the corner of Broadway and Ann Street, one of the Broadway Coach terminals, when she returned that evening. Later it would become known that he and Mary were engaged to be married.

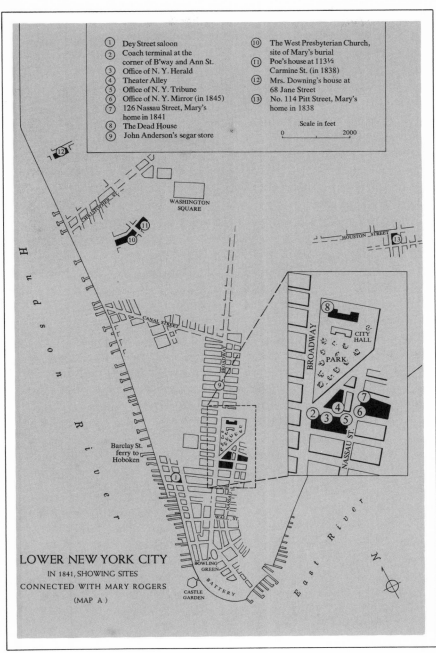

1. Dey Street saloon
2. Coach terminal at the corner of B'way and Ann St.
3. Office of N. Y. Herald
4. Theater Alley
5. Office of N. Y. Tribune
6. Office of N. Y. Mirror (in 1845)
7. 126 Nassau Street, Mary's home in 1841
8. The Dead House
9. John Anderson's segar store
10. The West Presbyterian Church, site of Mary's burial
11. Poe's house at 113½ Carmine St. (in 1838)
12. Mrs. Downing's house at 68 Jane Street
13. No. 114 Pitt Street, Mary's home in 1838

Scale in feet
0   2000

WASHINGTON SQUARE

Hudson River

CHRISTOPHER ST.

HOUSTON STREET

CANAL STREET

Barclay St. ferry to Hoboken

BROADWAY

CITY HALL

PARK

NASSAU ST.

WALL ST.

BOWLING GREEN

BATTERY

CASTLE GARDEN

East River

N

LOWER NEW YORK CITY
IN 1841, SHOWING SITES
CONNECTED WITH MARY ROGERS
(MAP A)

Christie McFall

At approximately 11 A.M. Payne left the house and visited his brother's home in Warren Street. At 1 P.M. he went to a saloon in Dey Street; at 2 P.M. he dined in a Fulton Street restaurant; he reached home at 3 P.M., and rested until 6, when he strolled the half mile to the Battery and met his brother again. By 7 P.M. he was waiting for Mary at the Ann Street terminal—but a violent thunderstorm which had been threatening all afternoon finally broke, and Payne, surmising from past experience that Mary would not attempt a return in such weather, retreated to the Dey Street saloon once more. By 9 P.M. he was back at the Nassau Street house where Mary's aunt, Mrs. Hays, agreed with him that the girl would have stayed the night at Jane Street. Payne went to bed with a clear conscience—but it was the last untroubled day he would ever know.[26]

On Monday he went to his job in a cork factory. Home for lunch, he was told that Mary still had not been heard from or seen. He took the fifteen-minute stage ride to Jane Street, only to discover that Mrs. Downing had not been at home on Sunday and could tell him nothing about the girl. For the rest of the day Payne anxiously visited the homes of Mary's friends and relatives in Harlem, Williamsburg (a village on the Brooklyn shore), and Staten Island. But he could find nothing; Mary had vanished. Early next morning, he received a note from a tavern on Duane Street, informing him that a young girl and her escort had been there on Sunday, but inquiry proved the girl could not have been Mary. Leaving the tavern, Payne crossed the Hudson to Hoboken, then the playground of New Yorkers, where he made careful inquiries at the ferry-house, at three homes near the landing, and at the Elysian Fields, an open, grassy area much favored for lounging, band music and athletics. Again his efforts were fruitless.[27] He returned to the city and went to the office of the New York *Sun,* where he placed a disguised notice asking for information. It appeared the next day:

> Left her home on Sunday morning, July 25th, a young lady, had on a white dress, black shawl, blue scarf, leghorn hat, light colored shoes and parasol light colored; it is supposed some accident has befallen her. Whoever will give information respecting her at 126 Nassau Street shall be rewarded for their trouble.[28]

Alfred Crommeline, who had boarded with Mrs. Rogers until a

month previously, and who had been a suitor of Mary's until the advent of Payne, had heard on both Monday and Tuesday that excitement prevailed over Mary's whereabouts. When he read the veiled notice in the *Sun* on Wednesday, he became thoroughly alarmed. He went first to see Mrs. Rogers, then to the Police Office to enlist the aid of a friend who, however, proved unavailable. He then rechecked the Duane Street tavern. At this point, he later explained, he came to a chilling conclusion: Mary, he felt, might have been abducted for immoral purposes and perhaps was even then being held prisoner—possibly in some house of assignation across the Hudson. About midday of the 28th, Crommeline, with his friend Archibald Padley, also a former lodger at the house on Nassau Street, took the ferry to Hoboken. The two men asked questions at the landing and walked along the shore path to the Elysian Fields. Then, near the site of Sybil's Cave, at Castle Point, the search for Mary Rogers came to an abrupt end. Spying a small crowd milling at the water's edge, Crommeline pushed forward and found himself staring down at the bedraggled body of a young girl lying on the sand.

A *Herald* reporter, on the scene by coincidence, later provided this description of the sight that met Crommeline's eyes: "The first look we had of her was most ghastly. Her forehead and face appeared to have been battered and butchered to a mummy. Her features were scarcely visible, so much violence had been done to her. On her head she wore a bonnet—light gloves on her hands, with the long watery fingers peering out—her dress was torn in various portions—her shoes were on her feet—and altogether she presented the most horrible spectacle that the eye could see."[29] Despite the altered facial appearance, Crommeline knew it was Mary. He recognized her clothes, and he remembered a hairiness on her arms—a characteristic also displayed by the pitiful body on the sand, though he had to rub the lifeless arm to be sure.

A Coroner's inquest, presided over by Justice Gilbert Merritt, was held that evening in Hoboken, after Dr. Richard Cook had examined the body. The jury needed no time to deliberate but promptly rendered a decision that the death was the result of "violence committed by some person or persons unknown."[30] Crommeline found it necessary to spend the night in nearby Jersey

City, since the ferries had stopped running before the inquest had
finished, but he had earlier sent Padley back to carry the heavy news
to Mary's mother.[31] The next day Crommeline returned to New
York carrying bits of the clothing and a lock of the dark hair for
further identification.

Newspaper reaction was matter-of-fact at first, probably because
the body had been found in New Jersey waters and the Hoboken
Police Office had assumed charge of the case.[32] The first word
filtered into New York through the *Commercial Advertiser* which,
on July 29th, printed a few noncommittal lines about the inquest.
On the 31st the *Herald* provided some additional details, but the
account was still buried with more mundane items under the
standing head "Police Office." On August 1st both the *Herald* and
the New York *Mercury* suddenly elevated Mary's death to the status
of major news, and from that time on her name was not out of
public attention for more than a day at a time, full-scale coverage of
the case lasting for six weeks.[33]

Not everyone, however, was in sympathy with the dead girl. The
New York *Advocate of Moral Reform* took the opportunity to drive
home a lesson: "One word to the young ladies into whose hands this
paper may fall . . . a voice from the grave—from an untimely and
dishonored grave—speaks to you in tones of warning and entreaty.
Had Cecilia Rogers loved the house of God—had she reverenced the
Sabbath—had she refused to associate with unprincipled and
profligate men—how different had been her fate!"[34] All of which was
the fever point of moral fervor, since there was no evidence that
Mary didn't reverence the house of God, and not the slightest clue
regarding her companions at the time of her death.

On August 11th, at the request of New York's acting mayor
Elijah Purdy, the body was exhumed from its temporary Hoboken
grave for more positive identification by her mother, and taken to
the Dead House, behind New York's City Hall. Here Mrs. Rogers
came to look on her daughter for the last time, but the condition of
the body mercifully prevented such an inspection. Instead, she was
shown the rest of Mary's clothes, especially the long white dress,
now no longer quite so white, and identification was complete:
"The magistrates yesterday had the body recognized beyond the
shadow of a doubt . . . . Phoebe Rogers says that she has seen the

dress taken from the body and that it is the clothing of Mary Cecilia Rogers and the same she wore on Sunday the 25th July."[35] The next day Mary was reinterred in a small cemetery behind the West Presbyterian Church, which then stood at the northern terminus of Varick Street.[36] But even here the girl did not find her final rest. Years later, when Seventh Avenue was extended southward to connect with Varick, the church was demolished. Soon afterwards, the cemetery where Mary lay was incorporated into a neighboring park, and such bodies as could be located were transferred to newer burial grounds on Long Island. The mortal remains of the Beautiful Cigar Girl have vanished forever, it would appear, even if her name has continued to glitter in the light of reflected immortality.

CHAPTER TWO

The terrible Murder of Miss
Rogers excites daily a deeper
and wider interest in our
city. Well may it do so . . .

New York *Tribune,*
August 6, 1841

The Unsolved Case

MARY'S lifeless body had been discovered floating in the
waters of the Hudson off Castle Point, a promontory
just north of Hoboken. Two men in a boat had pulled
alongside, thinking at first the object was a bundle of
rags; realizing it was a body, they had fixed a rope to it and pulled it
ashore.[1] It had been lying on the sand perhaps a half hour when
Crommeline and Padley arrived.

The cause of death, as announced at the inquest by Dr. Cook, was
strangulation after sexual abuse. Mary, he explained, had been tied,
gagged, raped by at least three men, had then been throttled and
thrown into the river. The telltale gag still hung loosely on her neck
when she was found, and her frail wrists retained the excoriations of
the ropes. Bound tightly in the flesh of her neck, underneath the
gag, Cook had found a thin strip of lace trimming that had been
torn from her dress. This, he stated, had caused her death.[2]

Both press and police immediately laid the crime to one of the
many New York gangs that infested the Hoboken area on weekends,
and that supposition was strengthened by stories of a young girl, or
girls, having been seen at various hours of the fatal Sunday

23

consorting with "fire-rowdies and soaplocks" along the Weehawken shore. Names were obtained from witnesses and some preliminary arrests were made, but these early suspects easily cleared themselves.

Several chance phrases in Dr. Cook's report next sent the police after William Kiekuck, Mrs. Rogers' former boarder, a common sailor then serving aboard the receiving ship *North Carolina* in the Brooklyn Navy Yard. In alluding to the strings of the dead girl's bonnet, Cook had said they were tied in "a slip knot; not a lady's knot. In a sailor's knot. . . ." In referring to a strip of skirt that had been twined around her waist, he had described it as "secured by a sort of hitch in the back."[3] These things seemed to indicate a seaman, and when witnesses came forward who claimed they saw Mary on the day of her disappearance meet a young man, "apparently an acquaintance," in Theater Alley, around the corner from her house on Nassau Street, the police began to think the case was near solution. Kiekuck was taken from the *North Carolina,* on suspicion, but after "long and critical interrogatories by the Magistrate," he was released. Suspicion of him lingered, however, and he was questioned again on August 12th, when he was made to give a circumstantial account of his time, both before and after Mary's death.[4] Eventually he was able to convince the police that he had not seen the girl since July 3d. Payne, Crommeline and Padley also were closely questioned more than once, but they too presented affidavits that established their innocence.[5]

The gang theory remained prevalent throughout the investigation, but there was from the start some idea that Mary could have been the victim of an abortion attempt. The possibility was not at first discussed openly, but by the middle of August several papers felt called upon to deny such rumors.[6] Dr. Cook, on the 16th, publicly stated that she "had evidently been a person of chastity and correct habits . . . there was not the slightest trace of pregnancy."[7] His opinion, however, did not convince many, and a number of papers promptly labeled as "sentiment" his notion that Mary had been subjected to repeated sexual attack, a fact difficult if not impossible to establish from a belated physical examination.

Through the early days of August public excitement continued to build, with the Jersey shore attracting more than its usual number of sojourners. "The curiosity and crowds still continue at

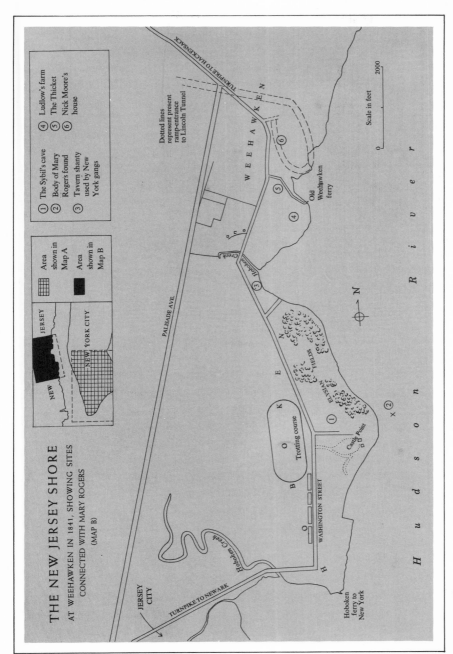

THE NEW JERSEY SHORE

AT WEEHAWKEN IN 1841, SHOWING SITES
CONNECTED WITH MARY ROGERS
(MAP B)

① The Sybil's cave
② Body of Mary Rogers found
③ Tavern shanty used by New York gangs
④ Ludlow's farm
⑤ The Thicket
⑥ Nick Moore's house

Area shown in Map A
Area shown in Map B

NEW JERSEY
NEW YORK CITY

Dotted lines represent present ramp-entrance to Lincoln Tunnel

Scale in feet
0   2000

W E E H A W K E N

TURNPIKE TO HACKENSACK

PALISADE AVE.

Hoboken Creek

Old Weehawken ferry

N

Trotting course

H O B O K E N

ELYSIAN FIELDS

Castle Point

WASHINGTON STREET

Hoboken ferry to New York

TURNPIKE TO NEWARK

JERSEY CITY

Hoboken Creek

H u d s o n   R i v e r

Christie McFall

Hoboken—and the name of poor Mary Rogers is on every lip," the *Herald* reported. Business enterprise was not lacking. A daguerreotypist named Baker, of 8 Wall Street, managed to procure a miniature of the girl from which he produced a "correct likeness of Miss Rogers." Advertising his handwork in the *Sun,* he urged: "A pedlar might sell a great number by taking them to Hoboken, where so many persons are visiting the spot daily."[8] At this time photography was scarcely more than one year old, and Baker must be given credit for his enterprise in so quickly finding a commercial use for the new technique. The pamphleteers required rather longer to throw together their own product, but by August 11th New Yorkers were informed that inside knowledge of the murder at long last was available:

> THAT DARK DEED—The life and murder of Mary C. Rogers will be published at the office of the Sunday *Times,* this morning in pamphlet form, with a splendid full-length portrait, declared to be a perfect likeness, with further particulars of the murder, the knowledge of which is confined to the police and the writer of this pamphlet—nine persons Broadway gamblers supposed to be concerned in the murder. The life is full of interest—it contains an account of several attempts of courtship and seduction brought about by her manifold charms. Office 31 Ann St.—Price six cents.[9]

In such an atmosphere, confusion and rumor abounded. It was said that the body found in the river wasn't Mary's, that the girl was still alive and had returned home; it was doubted that the murder had been perpetrated in New Jersey at all, but that the girl had met her death in New York, and the body thrown into the river, whence it had floated to the opposite shore. It was argued variously that the cause of death was strangulation or drowning, and disagreement soon began over the length of time it would take a drowned body to rise to the surface. It was even whispered that the girl had, for some dark reason, taken her own life. Witnesses came forward who swore that they had seen Mary arguing with a young man near the Elysian Fields on the day of her disappearance; anonymous letters reached the police voicing suspicion in different directions, and almost all the city's papers expressed impatience with the slowness of the authorities. This welter of excited public interest resolved itself, on August 11th, into a meeting of private citizens.

About thirty people, including writer-editor Richard Adams

Locke, gathered at the house of James C. Stoneall, 29 Ann Street, where they were "eloquently addressed" by five or six speakers, who reminded their hearers that "within the last few years seven murders have been committed within this city, for the perpetration of which no one has been brought to punishment."[10] A Committee of Safety was formed to aid the police and a reward of $500 announced, with the statement that it was hoped soon to raise it to $1,000. The money had been pledged by more than a hundred citizens, among whom were many of the editors of the city's newspapers and periodicals as well as Mary's neighbors. John Anderson and James Gordon Bennett topped the list with contributions of $50 each.

The meeting seems to have precipitated official action, for two days later Mayor Purdy took personal control of the investigation, sending for all records and ordering a hearing for the purpose of reexamining Dr. Cook of Hoboken. Reporters were admitted to the hearing held on August 16th, but, unfortunately for posterity, were directed by the Mayor to confine their reports to general statements. The *Herald* the following day tantalized its readers with the information that it possessed "full notes of the whole of the testimony; but, under the directions of His Honor, we, of course, suppress all that portion of it, the publication of which would be calculated to defeat the ends of public justice."[11] Then it promptly proceeded to supply virtually an entire column of questions and answers. Nothing new, however, was developed by the hearing.

Shortly after the mayor's hearing there was a brief flurry of excitement in which it seemed to many people that the murderer had been apprehended. One Joseph Morse, an engraver who lived a few doors from the Rogers house, soon after the announcement of Mary's death, abused his wife and left the city. The woman filed a complaint with the police who found him hiding in Worcester, Massachusetts, where he had bought new clothes and shaved off his beard. On August 15th he was arrested and brought back to New York, where the papers, on the 18th, revealed the new development with all the air of a denouement. To police, Morse admitted picking up a young girl on the Sunday of Mary's disappearance and taking her to Staten Island, where he kept her overnight and tried unsuccessfully to seduce her. He left the girl on Staten Island in disgust that day, he insisted, but when he read later in the week of

the Rogers murder, he surmised not illogically that his reluctant
companion might have been the dead girl. He took fright, argued
with his wife and ran. For a day or two following the announcement
of these facts, it appeared that the whole city, led by the innuendos
of the press, agreed on Morse's guilt, but the young lady in question
came forward dramatically to corroborate the story, and by August
20 Morse was cleared.[12]

Though the mystery remained a leading item, it was again
without a clue and bogged in rumors and second guesses, and
nothing of real interest developed as August wore into the first week
of September. New York Governor William Seward added $750 to
the reward money, and the New York Board of Aldermen briefly
considered raising it by another $500, but the motion was voted
down.[13] Seward also offered a pardon to any accomplice who would
come forward, but five weeks had passed with police no nearer a
solution, and the feeling began to spread that neither rewards nor
pardons were likely to prove effective.[14] It is possible, however, that
the development that now occurred actually did come as an indirect
result of the reward offer, which stood at $1,250. If it did, its effects,
for literature at any rate, were far-reaching.

The break in the case did not occur in any sudden or dramatic
way. This part of the story—the finding of some of Mary's clothes at
the supposed site of the murder—has always been the most confused
and misunderstood element in the entire case. It is possible,
however, to reconstruct the sequence of events pretty much as they
unrolled within the knowledge first of the authorities and then the
public.[15]

Sometime during the last days of August, Mrs. Frederica Loss,
proprietor of a roadhouse near the shore at Weehawken, informed
the Hoboken police that her sons had found some articles of
women's clothing strewn around the cramped interior of a dense
thicket about 300 yards from her establishment. Included were a
parasol, a handkerchief marked with the name of Mary Rogers (or
the initials M. R.; the accounts conflict), a silk scarf, a pair of
gloves, and, rather puzzlingly, a white petticoat. There were also
two small strips of cloth clinging to one of the briar bushes. Mrs.
Loss had immediately recognized the scarf as belonging to a young

girl who had been at her inn on the Sunday of Mary's
disappearance. In company with "a dark complexioned young
man," Mrs. Loss said, the girl had arrived at the inn about 4 P.M.,
had taken some lemonade and had departed on the arm of her
companion a half hour later. She had impressed Mrs. Loss by her
"affable and modest behavior," and the woman had noted the
similarity of the girl's dress to one owned by her sister. The girl, she
remarked, had smiled and bowed prettily as she left. Soon after
dark, or about 9 P.M., Mrs. Loss had sent one of her sons to drive a
bull down the shore road to a farm known as Ludlow's:

> Sometime after he left she heard what she calls a frightful screaming as of
> a young girl in great distress, partly choked and calling for assistance, and
> sounded like "Oh! oh! God!" etc., uttered in great agony. So loud were the
> screams that her other son heard them down in the cellar. She thought the
> bull had gored her boy, and rushed out in terror, calling his name down
> the road to Ludlow's. As soon as she called out, there was a noise as of
> struggling, and a stifled, suffering scream and then all was still.[16]

Mrs. Loss hurried on to Ludlow's farm, found her boy safe, and
returned to the inn. She dismissed the screams: there had been a
much larger crowd of weekenders than usual on the shore that
Sunday, including the ever troublesome "fire-rowdies, butcher-boys,
soap-locks, and all sorts of riotous miscreants." More than one noisy
fight had broken out among the three or four gangs that had rowed
over from the city and congregated at the "rum hole on the mud
bank." It was just a month afterwards, Mrs. Loss told police, that
her boys had found Mary's things in the thicket.

Almost miraculously, no hint of these disclosures reached the
papers, and on September 5th, after some preliminary investigation
at Weehawken, the New York police officially requested a news
blackout. The editor of every paper in the city received a copy of
the letter:

Police Office, Sept. 5th, 1841

> Sir: I am requested by the Magistrate of the Lower P. O. to request you to
> suspend the publication of anything relative to the murder of Mary C.
> Rogers for the present. The reason will be given to your reporter
> tomorrow.

Respectfully Yours,
B. W. Osborn, Clerk[17]

Contemporary sketch of the Loss Inn,
known as the Nick Moore House, at Weehawken.
Published in the New York *Herald,*
September 17, 1841

Courtesy of The New-York Historical Society, New York City

This came a fraction too late, however. The *Herald* had succeeded
in rooting out some minimum facts, and on September 6th it
reported briefly that Mary's "shawl and parasol" had been found "in
a tavern at Weehawken." By the 7th, it had learned nearly the
entire story, but the blackout request, honored by all the other
papers, made things awkward, though not, of course, to the point of
total silence. In a terse paragraph the *Herald* assured its readers it
knew "all the horrible facts which have recently been discovered,"
told of the finding of the clothes in the thicket, and concluded that
Mary had undoubtedly been violated and murdered by a gang.
"When we are permitted," it promised, "we will lift the veil, and
show scenes of blood and brutality, that will make the hair stand on
end." But then even the *Herald* fell silent, and for ten days New
Yorkers heard no more of Mary Rogers.

Even these fragmentary revelations, however, had enhanced the
curiosity value of Hoboken and Weehawken, and the crowds
continued to drift across the river and wander up and down the
shore. One such sightseer was the writer Lydia Maria Child,
temporarily a resident of the city and preparing a volume to be
called *Letters from New York*. She could hardly overlook
Weehawken as a subject for a letter and a pinch of moralizing, but
she was careful to heighten the drama of her account by viewing it
in the desolation of night. With a companion, she went there,
probably on September 7th:

> Last week I again saw Hoboken in the full glory of moonlight. Seen thus,
> it is beautiful beyond imagining. The dark, thickly shaded groves, where
> the flickering shadows play fantastic gambols with the moonlight . . .
> about three miles from the landing place, you arrive at Weehawken . . . .
> One of the last places that should be desecrated by the evil passions of man.
> It is as lovely as a nook of Paradise, before Satan entered its gardens . . . .
> We descended to return to the steamboat, by an open path on the river's
> edge. The high bank, among whose silent groves we had been walking, now
> rose above our heads in precipitous masses of rugged stone, here and there
> broken into recesses, which, in the evening light, looked like darksome
> caverns. Trees bent over the very edge of the summit, and their unearthed
> roots twisted among the rocks like huge serpents. On the other side lay the
> broad Hudson in the moonlight, its waves rippling up to the shore with a
> cool, refreshing sound. All else was still—still—so fearfully still, that one
> might almost count the beatings of the heart. That my heart did beat I

acknowledge; for here was the supposed scene of the Mary Rogers tragedy; and though the recollection of *her* gave me no uneasiness, I could not forget that the quiet, lovely, path we were treading was near to the city, with its thousand hells, and frightfully easy of access. We spoke of the murdered girl, as we passed the beautiful promontory near the Sybil's Cave where her body was found lying half in and half out of the water. A few steps further on we encountered the first human beings we had met during the whole of our long ramble—two young women singing with somewhat sad constraint, as if to keep their courage up. I had visited the Sybil's Cave in the daytime, and should have entered its dark mouth by moonlight, had not the aforesaid remembrances of the city haunted me like evil spirits.[18]

During the ten days of newspaper silence James Gordon Bennett did not, it appears, allow the *Herald* reporters to rest. On September 17th he defied the wishes of the police, and broke the tension with a lengthy article on the Weehawken finds and Mrs. Loss's testimony. Prominent across two columns of the second page of the paper was an engraving in which was depicted the Loss inn (known locally as the Nick Moore House), with the information that it was "The House Where Mary Rogers Was Last Seen Alive." The story revealed that Mary had been recognized crossing to Hoboken by two men who knew her. One was Adam Wall, the driver of the stage that met the ferry, who had also recognized her corpse on the following Wednesday; the other man was not named. The narrative supplied by Mrs. Loss—"a fine, intelligent, good-looking lady, about thirty years of age, and of German descent"—was given in detail, and much was made of the packs of hoodlums that had roamed the Weehawken groves that Sunday. Especially remembered was one gang of fifteen which had noisily visited "the little shanty by the roadside, next to Nick Moore's house, seized all the cakes, etc., and ate them—refused to pay anything, and threatened to beat anybody that interfered with them." These ruffians, said the *Herald,* had remained prowling about until after dark, when they departed in a hurry. The details of the finding of the clothes in the thicket were presented at length:

> Time passed on until the 25th of last month. On that day [Mrs. Loss's] boys were out collecting sassafras bark, and chanced to penetrate the small thicket between the two roads, on the side of the hill where the murder was committed. Here there are three or four very large stones, forming a kind of seat, with back and footstool to it. The boughs and briar bushes

are twined thickly around it, and there is not room scarcely to stand upright in it. In fact it is a place fit for such a murder, and one from which the unfortunate girl could not have escaped without violation, if ever she was forced into it. On the upper stone lay a white garment. The little boy exclaimed "Halloo, there's somebody has left their shirt." The big boy picked it up and found it was a woman's petticoat. On the second stone lay the identical silk scarf (all crumpled up, as if torn off forcibly), which was worn by the young lady who was at Mrs. Loss's house, and which has been identified as Mary Rogers' scarf. The petticoat had been darned in a hurry, and that has been identified. In a little hollow between the seat stone and a trunk of a small tree, lay Mary Rogers' parasol, and pocket handkerchief, marked with her name. A little further off lay her gloves, turned inside out, as if they had been forcibly drawn from her hands in a hurry. And on one of the briar bushes, hung two pieces of her dress which had evidently been torn out, as she was dragged through this horrid place; one piece of the dress was so doubled as to have a thorn three times through it. The place around was stamped about, and the branches were broken, and roots bruised and mashed, all betokening that it had been the scene of a very violent struggle. The marks of a high heeled boot were very plain. And it appeared from the position of the articles, as if the unfortunate girl had been placed upon the middle broad stone, her head held forcibly back, and then and there horribly violated by several rowdies, and ultimately strangled. The spot is not far from the river—the access to the water easy—and the rails between it and the river were all found taken down, as if the bodies of Mary Rogers and the young man*, had both been carried thence from the scene of the murder. In order that it may not be supposed that these things were placed there recently, it is proper to state, that from their appearance this could not have been the case. The things had all evidently been there at least three or four weeks. They were all mildewed down hard from the action of the rain, and stuck together from the mildew. The grass had grown around and over some of them. The silk and the parasol were strong, but the threads of it were run together, within the upper part where it had been doubled and folded was all mildewed and rotten, and tore on its being opened. The white linen handkerchief had a corded border around it and was mildewed also. So was the scarf. This and the petticoat were crumpled up, as if in a struggle. The pieces of her frock torn out by the bushes were about three inches wide and six inches long. One part was the hem of the frock, and it had been mended; the other piece was part of the skirt, not the hem. They looked like strips torn off, and were on the thorn bush about a foot from the ground. The petticoat, shawl, etc., were full of little bugs, called by the Dutch, kellerasbe, that is, in English, cellar jackass, an insect that always gets into clothing lying in wet places.[19]

*The *Herald* was theorizing that a gang had killed both Mary and her escort.

All of these articles of clothing, said the *Herald*, had been carefully gathered by Mrs. Loss and taken to the police at the earliest opportunity. The paper failed, however, to emphasize the most important point of all: the description of the clothes in the thicket, and their appearance when found, had been supplied by Mrs. Loss. *No one else saw the clothes in place,* not even the police. The *Herald*'s oversight, perhaps, is understandable; no other paper picked it up, and its significance has escaped all subsequent writers on the case. In any event, it would not become apparent till later. In the meantime, the *Herald* assured its readers that it had additional facts and "inferences" that would shortly be forthcoming.

True to its word, on the following Tuesday, September 21, it printed another lengthy article, again headed by a two-column woodcut, this time the interior of the thicket, captioned "The Actual Spot Where the Shocking Murder and Violation of Mary Rogers Took Place." The story, however, was only a bluff. It offered no new facts, but stretched itself over descriptions of the thicket, more talk of the gangs that had disturbed the neighborhood on the

Contemporary sketch of the thicket at
Weehawken in which, supposedly,
the murder of Mary Rogers took place.
Published in the New York *Herald*,
September 21, 1841

Contemporary sketch of the shore at Weehawken,
published in the New York *Herald,* September 24,
1841. The paper supplied the following identification
for the lettering: A—entrance to the murder thicket;
B—an old disused road; C—lane running to the
Nick Moore House; D—tavern shanty frequented by
New York gangs; E—north point of the Elysian Fields;
F—Castle Point, at southern end of Elysian Fields;
G—point on shore where the *Herald* conjectured
Mary's body had been put into a rowboat to be
carried to deep water

fatal day, much pointless speculation, and frequent decrying of "the
dreadful deed." With McDonald Clarke's verses on "The Beautiful
Segar Girl" prominently displayed, it concluded by calling on the
police to "find out what boats and what crews were over at
Weehawken that day." The paper brought its expose to a close with
a front-page splash three days later that offered yet another look at
the murder ground—a sweeping view of the Weehawken shore, the
thicket, the path by the river, and New York in the distance. The
accompanying article, however, again failed to add anything new,
and busied itself with refuting some of the doubts that had started
to circulate.

> It is worse than idle, on the part of many persons who ought to know
> better, to attempt to throw a doubt over the locality of the murder of this
> poor girl. It was undoubtedly done at Weehawken. The spot already
> described as the thicket is comparatively close to the river. The route from
> it to the river can be traveled even in the day time, frequently without
> meeting a single soul, much less in the night. The spot is just an one
> as would be selected for such a murder. After dark, it frequently happens
> that not a soul passes that place by the hour together. A thousand persons
> may pass the spot even now, and not notice it. . . . So much then for the
> silly statement that the articles must have been recently put there or they
> would have been discovered before.[20]

By now, though, the paper had become less certain as to the exact
manner of Mary's death. It couldn't make up its mind if she had
been the victim of a gang of rowdies, who had also done for her
dark-complexioned escort, or if she had been murdered in a fit of
passion by her solitary companion. The young man, it speculated,

> . . . might have been attempting to take liberties with her; she resisted and
> screamed; he choked her, dragged her into the thicket, and there violated
> and murdered her. Then stayed by the dead and mangled body of his
> victim, in that dark thicket, with no eye but that of God upon the
> murderer and the murdered maid, until all was still—perhaps till near
> midnight. Then tying the frock around her to form a handle, he carried
> her to the river, and hurled her in, and fled, too horror stricken to think of
> returning to the scene of the murder, to remove the articles found by the
> boys.[21]

But this promising discovery at Weehawken, disappointingly,
ended in nothing. The police, of course, questioned Mrs. Loss and
her boys, studied the articles of clothing, spoke to others who had
been at Weehawken on the 25th, scoured the thicket area, and
certainly must have questioned known gangs in the city. None of
this led anywhere, and by the time the excitement of the *Herald*
articles had worn off, the Mary Rogers case had come to the end of
its moment of fame. There were infrequent, incidental references
during the remainder of September, but in the absence of fresh
news it had lost its hold on the public.

Before it quite evaporated, however, it dragged down another
pathetic victim. On October 7th, Daniel Payne, haggard and
worried looking, called at the Loss inn, and inquired the location of
the thicket in which Mary supposedly had met her death. He then
drank some brandy and left. He was seen that day and the next

wandering aimlessly around the Weehawken environs, calling at various public houses and continuing to drink heavily. Once or twice he was found stretched on the ground, and helped to his feet, and towards evening on the 8th, he was discovered lying face down in a stupor, on a bench near Castle Point. A doctor was called who pronounced him dead a few moments later. In his pocket was a penciled note: "To the World—Here I am on the spot; God forgive me for my misfortune in my misspent time." Near the thicket, searchers afterwards picked up an empty phial of laudanum, and within the thicket they found Payne's hat, on which the bereaved young man had wound a band of black crepe.[22]

CHAPTER THREE

Upon reading these various extracts,
they not only seemed to me irrelevant,
but I could perceive no mode in which
any one of them could be brought to
bear upon the matter in hand. I waited
for some explanation from Dupin.

The narrator in
The Mystery of Marie Roget

Mary Rogers Becomes *Marie*

THE MYSTERY OF MARIE ROGET marks the second
appearance of Poe's detective, the Chevalier C. Auguste
Dupin, and the story thus occupies a peculiarly important
position in the history of detective fiction. It becomes an
interesting speculation, then, as to why Poe chose an actual, current,
unsolved case for his hero's return. Dupin's first case, *The Murders
in the Rue Morgue,* had also taken its rise from a real incident,[1] but
the plot as Poe developed it was entirely imaginary. Certainly he
could have easily found another theme suitable for the further
display of Dupin's powers without tying himself so rigidly to the
necessities, and uncertainties, of known fact. Poe himself gave no
reason for his choice, but it is just possible that his bold action may
have been undertaken in response to a challenge. The sparkling
ingenuity he had exhibited in *The Murders in the Rue Morgue* had
aroused admiration, but this had soon been tempered by a feeling
that the cleverness was synthetic: what ability, it was rather naively
asked, was required to solve a mystery that had, in the first place,
been built up by the solver? This idea was advanced by more than
one commentator at the time, and as late as 1850 Poe's literary

39

executor Rufus Griswold repeated it in the *Memoir* published with his edition of Poe's works.[2] Did some Philadelphia friend of Poe's—perhaps Henry B. Hirst, the young lawyer-writer who was so constant a companion at this time—urge or dare him to exercise his talents on an actual mystery? The possibility is not far-fetched; it was just the sort of challenge that Poe would have responded to with bravado—and the dark fate of poor Mary was ready to hand. In fact, it is well within the bounds of possibility that Hirst or some other friend may have specifically suggested the Rogers case as a suitable theme.[3]

The final newspaper echoes of the real murder had sounded on October 11, 1841, with the report of Payne's suicide, and *The Mystery of Marie Roget* was complete by the end of May, 1842. Seven months separate the two dates, but there exists no indication as to when the story was begun or how long Poe worked at it. He was, of course, busy with other things during this time, and was also still editing *Graham's,* by then one of the leading popular magazines in the country. He could hardly have begun a story on the theme of Mary Rogers, it is clear, until the case had definitely become dormant, and this certainly would not have been evident until well into 1842.

His personal life at the time he was writing *Marie Roget* had become sadly tangled and burdensome. His wife Virginia suffered her first consumptive hemorrhage in mid-January, 1842, and her life was at first despaired of. She recovered but continued to linger in an ebb and flow of strength during the remainder of the year. By the end of March, Poe had become fed up with his subordinate position on *Graham's* and had resigned, despite the fact that his finances, and Virginia's condition, seemingly permitted no such independent action. (In spite of rather general agreement that his resignation was prompted by inadequate pay and broken promises, his leaving *Graham's* still remains one of the unexplained, and, in the circumstances, one of the least understandable actions of his life.[4]) Even in his resulting heavy pecuniary embarrassments, however, as his correspondence shows, he continued to promote his hopes for the *Penn Magazine*. What he and Virginia and Mrs. Clemm lived on during the months after his resignation from *Graham's* is problematic, and *The Mystery of Marie Roget* must be looked at in the context of his financial need. Perhaps, after all, he would not have attempted such a feat had it not been for the pressing necessities of his life at this time.

The tale did not take shape in an artistic vacuum but was, in fact, written at a time when Poe was especially immersed in formulating his thoughts on the comparatively new subject of literary detection. Throughout the entire period of the Mary Rogers case, as well as in the months just prior to the writing of *Marie Roget,* he was frequently occupied in mulling over the fundamentals of the new literary genre he had crystalized in *The Murders in the Rue Morgue.* That story had appeared in *Graham's* for April, 1841, and in a letter of the following July 12th Poe referred with satisfaction to its popularity. Earlier, on May 1, 1841, there had appeared in the Philadelphia *Saturday Evening Post* his famous first review of a portion of Dickens' *Barnaby Rudge,* in which, supposedly, he had tried to anticipate the outcome of the Englishman's quasidetective story. The equally well known second *Rudge* review appeared in the February, 1842, issue of *Graham's*—though it must have been written no later than the previous December. These reviews, with their dissection of the mechanics of detective fiction, Poe was able to discuss with Dickens when the novelist, on his first American tour, arrived at Philadelphia in March 1842. They had two lengthy interviews at the United States Hotel about the 7th or 8th of that month.[5]

With the locale of the tale transferred to Paris, but with the name of Mary Cecilia Rogers prominently mentioned in the second paragraph, *The Mystery of Marie Roget* reconstructs the framework of the real case, altering only very minor and incidental details. He makes Marie twenty-two years old, for example, and has her work in a *parfumerie.* The Chevalier C. Auguste Dupin, still living in seclusion, is brought into the case by his friend, the Prefect G——of the Paris police. Dupin, of course, does not exert himself beyond his own door, and the pertinent facts are gathered for him by his companion, the unnamed narrator, who combs the newspaper accounts, visits police headquarters and finally presents Dupin with the results of his gleaning.

The first comment on the case offered by the detective is a variation on his famous dictum, originally given in *The Murders in*

Edgar Allan Poe in 1848
(The S. H. Whitman daguerreotype)

the Rue Morgue, in which he points out that extraordinary features
in a mystery do not, as is commonly thought, hinder a solution, but
instead make it more certain. The case of Marie Roget, on the other
hand, he remarks, is infinitely more difficult because of its
"especially *ordinary* character." Almost word for word, Dupin
repeats an aphorism he had earlier formulated in the *Rue Morgue:*
"It is by prominences above the plane of the ordinary, that reason
feels her way, if at all, in her search for the true." Having delivered
this, he spends much time in minute analysis of the various
discussions that had occupied the papers during the weeks when the
Rogers case was exciting New Yorkers, such as the question of the
identity of the corpse, and the behavior of drowned bodies in water.
This is compellingly done, but Poe adds nothing important, and for
the most part only rephrases the arguments, pro and con, that had
overflowed the newspaper columns.[6]

At this point, in a passage that anticipated the tone of a good deal of the detective fiction that followed, Dupin briefly explains his methods to his friend:

> In the analysis which I now propose, we will discard the *interior* points of this tragedy, and concentrate our attention upon its *outskirts*. Not the least usual error, in investigations such as this, is the limiting of inquiry to the immediate, with total disregard of the collateral or *circumstantial* events. It is the malpractice of the courts to confine evidence and discussion to the bounds of apparent *relevancy*. Yet experience has shown, and a true philosophy will always show, that a vast, perhaps the larger portion of truth arises from the seemingly irrelevant . . . .

Thus Poe sets the stage for his unorthodox and daring approach to a solution: the use of seemingly random newspaper accounts. To his companion, Dupin explains that he intends to turn his attention from "the event itself to the contemporary circumstances which surround it . . . . I will examine the newspapers more generally than you have as yet done. . . . It will be strange indeed if a comprehensive survey, such as I propose of the public prints, will not afford us some minute points which will establish a *direction* for inquiry."

After a week of solitary study, Dupin at length lays before his friend six extracts from various papers and proceeds to set forth his solution. Contrary to what is usually thought, these extracts were not verbatim quotations from contemporary newspapers, transferred intact by Poe from newsprint to the framework of his story. Four of them were compilations or adaptations, and the fifth was a close paraphrase of a single source. But the sixth seems to have had no basis at all in fact; it was invented by Poe to aid the impact of his tale's denouement.[7] In compiling and adapting the first five, it could be said, he had remained within an acceptable use of his sources—that is, the quotations he offered were "legitimate" in that they faithfully reflected contemporary reporting. The nonexistent sixth extract, however, was hardly playing fair, but, since it does not play a vital role in his solution, he may be forgiven the lapse.

Five of the six extracts were only incidental to his discussion— mere dressing—and only one had real importance. This was an item closely based on a specific story. Poe's adaptation runs:

> An evening journal of yesterday refers to a former mysterious
> disappearance of Mademoiselle Roget. It is well known that, during the
> week of her absence from Le Blanc's *parfumerie,* she was in the company
> of a young naval officer much noted for his debaucheries. A quarrel, as it is
> supposed, providentially led to her return home. We have the name of the
> Lothario in question, who is at present stationed in Paris, but for obvious
> reasons forbear to make it public.

Perhaps the main source for this was a long account in the *Herald* of
August 3, 1841, in which the following paragraph, already quoted
in connection with Mary's 1838 adventure, occurs:

> This young girl, Mary Rogers, was missing from Anderson's store three
> years ago for two weeks. It is asserted that she was then seduced by an
> officer of the U.S. Navy, and kept at Hoboken for two weeks. His name is
> well known on board his ship.

The vital element in this, for Poe, was the naval officer (he was, of
course, consciously rejecting the alternate explanations for Mary's
earlier disappearance). In his purest analytical strain, he proceeds to
build the probabilities, step by step. Dupin, explaining the
"irrelevant" newspaper stories to his friend, says that he has made
use of the "naval officer" extract

> chiefly to show you the extreme remissness of the police, who, as far as I
> can understand from the Prefect, have not troubled themselves in any
> respect, with an examination of the officer alluded to. Yet it is mere folly
> to say that between the first and second disappearance of Marie, there is no
> *supposable* connection. Let us admit the first elopement to have resulted in
> a quarrel between the lovers, and the return home of the betrayed. We are
> now prepared to view a second *elopement* (if we *know* that an elopement
> has again taken place) as indicating a renewal of the betrayer's advances,
> rather than as the result of new proposals by a second individual—we are
> prepared to regard it as a "making up" of the old *amour,* rather than as the
> commencement of a new one. The chances are ten thousand to one, that
> he who had once eloped with Marie would again propose an elopement,
> rather than that she to whom proposals of elopement had been made by
> one individual, should have them made to her by another.

Then, at just the right moment, Poe puts into Dupin's mouth a
classic bit of improvisation which seals his argument with a flourish:
"Let me call your attention to the fact, that the time elapsing
between the first ascertained, and the second supposed elopement, is
precisely the general period of the cruises of our men-of-war." The
statement, on the surface, is very effective. Usually it takes a second

or third reading to fully appreciate the implicit contradiction in the phrase "precisely the general period," and to realize that there could have been no set periods for the varied cruises of men-of-war—not to mention the fact that naval officers were occupied in many things besides sailing on warships. But it is a sally with the true Poe mastertouch.[8]

With much convoluted reasoning, Dupin refutes (largely by repeating newspaper discussion) the idea that a gang had done the murder. The traces of a struggle indicated by the arrangement of the clothes in the thicket, he insists, preclude the activities of a gang: "What struggle could have taken place—what so violent and enduring as to have left its 'traces' in all directions—between a weak and defenseless girl and the *gang* of ruffians imagined? The silent grasp of a few rough arms and all would have been over." The scene of the crime makes sense, he says, only "if we imagine but *one* violator." And why should a gang have left behind the evidence of Marie's clothes? This oversight, Dupin points out, was the "accident of an individual," too terror-stricken to return to the thicket after disposing of Marie's body in the river. Thus he comes round again to the naval officer.

Marie had been planning to elope with the officer, Dupin concludes, and the two caught in the rain at Weehawken had taken shelter in the thicket. There, Dupin surmises, the officer had violated Marie in a fit of passion and had then murdered her in a frenzy of guilt. "We are not forced to suppose a premeditated design of murder or of violation," Dupin sums up, "but there was the friendly shelter of the thicket, and the approach of rain—there was opportunity and strong temptation—and then a sudden and violent wrong, to be concealed only by one of darker dye." His final link to the naval officer was simple: the sailor's knot in Marie's bonnet strings, and the hitch in the strip of dress wound about her waist, both mentioned by Dr. Cook, as well as the dark complexion of the young escort described by Mrs. Loss. These things, says Dupin, "point to a seaman." But Poe's theory, of course, needed an officer, not an enlisted man, so Dupin continues: "His companionship with the deceased, a gay, but not an abject young girl, designates him as above the grade of the common sailor." This was rather lame and unconvincing but the flow of the narrative at this point just managed to sustain it, its lack of real meaning veiled in Poe's skillful use of the words "gay" and "abject." As a final, quite unnecessary, fillip he throws in a bit about tracing the boat used by the naval officer to dispose of Marie's body, which he pictures as accidentally being set adrift in the river. But this detail is based on the sixth newspaper extract, the invented one, and may be discarded as having no connection with the actual happenings.

In such a close blending of fact and fiction, Poe could hardly have provided the tale with the usual finale, showing the criminal brought to justice. Instead, he made use of a device in which the editor of the *Companion,* supposedly,[9] informs readers that he has taken the liberty of omitting the portion of the manuscript in which is described the apprehension of the killer, "for reasons which we shall not specify, but which to many readers will appear obvious." The spurious editorial note assures readers, however, that "an individual assassin was convicted, upon his own confession."*

The bulk of the writing on *Marie Roget* perhaps was done in April and May, and the story was ready for publication by the start of June. Ignoring both Philadelphia and New York, Poe offered it simultaneously to periodicals in widely separated cities. Under date of June 4th, he wrote to George Roberts, editor of the Boston *Notion:*

> My Dear Sir,
>
> It is just possible that you may have seen a tale of mine entitled "The Murders in the Rue Morgue," and published, originally, in "Graham's Magazine" for April 1841. Its *theme* was the exercise of ingenuity in the detection of a murderer. I have just completed a similar article, which I shall entitle "The Mystery of Marie Roget—A Sequel to the Murders in the Rue Morgue." The story is based upon the assassination of Mary Cecilia Rogers, which created so vast an excitement, some months ago in New-York. I have, however, handled my design in a manner altogether *novel* in literature. I have imagined a series of nearly exact coincidences occurring in Paris. A young grisette, one Marie Roget, has been murdered under precisely similar circumstances with Mary Rogers. Thus, under pretense of showing how Dupin (the hero of "The Rue Morgue") unravelled the mystery of Marie's assassination, I, in reality, enter into a very long and rigorous analysis of the New-York tragedy. No point is omitted. I examine, each by each, the opinions and arguments of the press upon the subject,

---

*Readers familiar with the story at this point will have noticed something awry. They are asked to read on in patience.

and show that this subject has been hitherto, *unapproached*. In fact, I believe not only that I have demonstrated not only the fallacy of the general idea—that the girl was the victim of a gang of ruffians—but have *indicated the assassin* in a manner which will give renewed impetus to investigation. My main object, nevertheless, as you will readily understand, is an analysis of the true principles which should direct inquiry in similar cases. From the nature of the subject, I feel convinced that the article will excite attention, and it has occurred to me that you would be willing to purchase it for the forthcoming Mammoth Notion. It will make 25 pages of Graham's Magazine; and, at the usual price, would be worth to me $100. For reasons, however, which I need not specify, I am desirous of having this tale printed in Boston, and, if you like it, I will say $50. Will you please write me upon this point?—by return of mail, if possible.[10]

A similar offer to Joseph Snodgrass, editor of the Baltimore *Saturday Visiter,* was also dated June 4th, and is couched in much the same terms, though the price is reduced to $40.[11] As it turned out, neither Roberts nor Snodgrass was sufficiently intrigued by Poe's promise to indicate the assassin, and the story was eventually taken by the *Ladies' Companion* of New York, then under the control of William Snowden, who had been interested enough in the Mary Rogers affair to contribute five dollars to the reward money.[12]

The tale ran some twenty thousand words in length, much too long for a single issue, and Snowden found it necessary to present it in three sections. The first instalment appeared in the *Companion* for November, indicating that Snowden could have bought it no later than early September, though it is probable the transaction took place much earlier than that. Correspondence, for example, shows that Poe was in New York on some unexplained business during the last days of June,[13] and it may have been at that time that the story was sold. It is obvious that, having completed the tale, Poe would be anxious to sell it and have it published as quickly as possible, since any new development in the Rogers case might easily invalidate all his careful efforts. Despite his subsequent peevish description of the *Companion* as "the *ne plus ultra* of ill-taste and vulgar humbuggery,"[14] he was undoubtedly glad enough to make the sale.

Whatever else it is, *The Mystery of Marie Roget,* considered solely as a composition, was an impressive feat for Poe to have

accomplished at this time. Beset by money worries, doubts about his future, and fears for his wife's health, it is somewhat surprising that he was able to bring the story to any sort of coherent close, especially in view of its minute complexity. Aside from the novels, it is the longest of his tales, and though its structure is at times weak and rambling, the reasoning on individual points is frequently tight and lucid.

The effort, however, told on him. In a letter of early June, written almost immediately after completion of the story, he confesses wearily that "the state of my mind has, in fact, forced me to abandon all mental exertion. The renewed and hopeless illness of my wife, ill health on my own part, and pecuniary embarrassments, have nearly driven me to distraction."[15] Unfortunately, there were further distractions awaiting him during that troublesome year of 1842.

Cover of the *Tragic Almanack* for 1843, showing Mary Rogers about to be hurled from a cliff, reflecting the early belief that she had been murdered by a gang

Courtesy of Thomas M. McDade

CHAPTER FOUR

Conscience, no longer able to
keep silence, breathes its
accusation into the ear of
Justice . . .

New York *Tribune*,
November 18, 1842

Incident at Weehawken

Toward the close of 1842 the great dream of Poe's life was
very near to realization: he had found a backer for the
magazine with which he had long hoped to play a leading
role in American letters. The formal agreement with
Thomas C. Clarke, of Philadelphia, was signed on January 31,
1843,[1] indicating that talks had begun toward the close of the
previous year. But the perverse fate that always seemed to hover
darkly in Poe's path now descended once more as—just at the
moment when he could glimpse the fulfillment of his most
cherished ambition—the ghost of Mary Rogers suddenly materialized
to threaten him with public ridicule.

Beginning on November 18, 1842, the New York papers, after
more than a year of silence, broke the case wide open again, and
intimated, as well, that the mystery was very near to solution. They
reported that Mrs. Loss, keeper of the Weehawken inn where Mary,
supposedly, was last seen alive, had been accidentally shot by one of
her sons and on her deathbed had, in some manner, disclosed the
fact that the girl had been the victim of a criminal abortion
performed at the inn. The most malevolent of fates could not have

51

timed all this any better. The first instalment of *Marie Roget*, in the
November issue of the *Companion*, had appeared in mid-October;
the second instalment, in the December issue, had gone on sale
about November 15, and the third instalment, with its closely
reasoned theory of first-degree murder by a naval officer, was
probably set in type. Poe, who had already endured months of
frustration in his resignation from *Graham's Magazine* and his
failure to obtain a promised government appointment, could hardly
have avoided being deeply disturbed by this threat to his reputation.
He would, perhaps, have been especially concerned about the use
certain of his New York critics would make of the sudden turn of
events (in particular Theodore S. Fay, author of *Norman Leslie,* a
popular novel also based on a New York murder, which Poe had
manhandled in a devastating and widely read review. During the
investigation of Mary Rogers' death, the earlier case had been
remembered and mentioned more than once in the papers.[2]). There
remains no record of what action Poe took in the predicament, but
a close study of the biographical background suggests a theory of
quite irresistible probability.

The five-week period in Poe's life between November 19 and
December 25, 1842, has always been a blank. His biographers,
without exception, pass over it in silence, assuming no doubt that he
was at home in Philadelphia hard at work on whatever writings he
later published. But it now seems more than likely that sometime in
late November Poe went to New York, where he made discreet
inquiries among his newspaper contacts along Nassau Street, and
perhaps also in the vicinity of Hoboken, and then made revisions in
the final instalment of the story *before* publication. Some good
reasons underlie this hypothesis, which will appear presently, but
for the moment it may be sufficient to record one significant fact:
the final instalment of the story did *not* appear in the January issue,
when it was to be expected, but was moved back, without
explanation, to the February issue. Thus *The Mystery of Marie
Roget* was started on a devious career which was to see its author
make further surreptitious revisions for the reprinting of the story
in the 1845 volume of *Tales,* and which has seen it enjoy a long and
totally absurd existence as one of the supreme examples of Poe's
analytical powers. But this anticipates. It is time now, while Poe

hurries to New York, for a closer look at the sudden developments at Weehawken early in November, 1842.

Mrs. Frederica Loss, owner and operator of the Nick Moore House, had dropped into relative obscurity soon after the last reverberations of Daniel Payne's sad death had subsided. She and her sons continued to dispense refreshments at the inn, her business no doubt increased by the recent notoriety. Then, without warning, the whole thing unraveled for Mrs. Loss forever.

The precise happenings of the first three weeks of November, while necessarily alluded to in most of the literature on the case, have never been fully understood nor reported; indeed even the papers of that day did not provide anything resembling full or consecutive accounts. A careful sifting, however, of all the information that is available makes it possible to draw a fairly

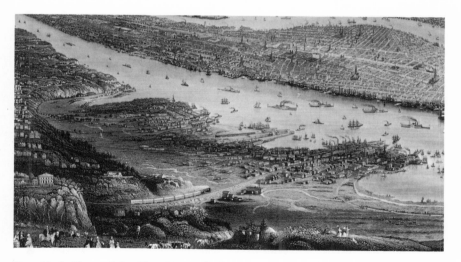

New York City and the New Jersey shore much as they looked at the time of Mary Rogers' death. The cluster of buildings in the right foreground is Jersey City. To the left along the shore are Hoboken and the Elysian Fields, and above them the cliffs of Weehawken. The view was made about 1867.

complete picture of events that have a crucial bearing on both the
Mary Rogers case and Poe's story.[3]

On November 1 or 2 Mrs. Loss was wounded by a shot from a
gun in the hands of her son. For nine days she lingered in delirium,
talking wildly in both English and German. At times, she imagined
she could see the spirit of some unidentified woman in her room,
and would cry out, "Shoo away! Shoo away!" or "Take her away!"
Sometime during this period, Justice Merritt visited the inn to
investigate the circumstances of the accident, and by November 4 or
5 rumors were circulating freely which definitely connected the
names of Mrs. Loss and Mary Rogers. Dr. Gautier, the Loss family
physician, was one of those who heard the rumors and shortly before
Mrs. Loss's death he performed an "experiment" that seems to have
come straight from the jurisprudence of the Middle Ages. Standing
over the dying woman he pronounced the name of Mary C. Rogers
"suddenly and loudly," and when "no effect was elicited" by this
procedure, Dr. Gautier concluded that she knew nothing more
about Mary's death. The rumors, however, were persistent, and they
included the supposedly inadvertent revelation, by one or more of
the Loss boys, that after their mother's death "the great secret would
come out." On November 10 Mrs. Loss succumbed to her wounds,
and the next day Merritt held an inquest which returned a verdict
of accidental death.

So far, no word of these happenings had reached the press, but on
November 12 the *Courier* published an account of the inquest,
though without mention of Mary Rogers:

> An inquest was held at Hoboken yesterday by Justice Gilbert Merritt of
> Hudson County, New Jersey, acting Coroner, on the body of Mrs. Frederica
> Loss, for some years the keeper of the "Nick Moon [sic] House" at the foot
> of Weehawken Hill, who came to her death by the accidental discharge of
> a gun held in the hands of one of her sons. Verdict of the Jury accordingly.[4]

After this, until November 18, the newspapers were silent on the
subject of Mrs. Loss's death—but judging by later developments,
there was much activity behind the scenes. Newspaper editors,
remembering Mrs. Loss's part in the investigation of the previous
year, immediately sent reporters to Hoboken and Weehawken to dig
deeper into the "accident." Such suspicion was well justified, for on
November 14 Justice Merritt, in a sworn affidavit, accused Mrs. Loss

and her three sons of complicity in the murder of Mary Rogers and the disposal of her body. Since this document has never been reprinted before,[5] though it is continually referred to in the Mary Rogers literature, it is given here in its entirety.

> *State of New Jersey Hudson Co.*—Personally appeared before me a Justice of the Peace, of said County, Gilbert Merritt, who being duly sworn by me, deposeth and saith:—that in the month of July 1841, he (this deponent) as a magistrate held an inquest on the body of Mary C. Rogers, at Hoboken, in said County of Hudson, who this deponent believes was murdered; and this deponent further saith that from information he has obtained and facts in his possession, he verily believes that the murder of the said Mary C. Rogers was perpetrated in a house at Weehawken, called "The Nick Moore House" then kept by one Frederica Loss, alias Kellenbarack (now deceased) and her three sons, to wit: Oscar Kellenbarack, Charles Kellenbarack, and Ossian Kellenbarack, all three of whom the deponent has reason to believe are worthless and profligate characters; and this deponent further saith, that he has just reason to believe that the said sons and their mother, kept one of the most depraved and debauched houses in New Jersey, and that all of them had a knowledge of and were accessory to, and became participators in the murder of said Mary C. Rogers, and the concealment of her body.
>
> Gilbert Merritt
>
> Sworn and subscribed the 14th of November, 1842, before me, Stephen H. Lutkins, Justice of the Peace.[6]

On the strength of this affidavit, the two eldest sons of Mrs. Loss were arrested and bound over for a judicial hearing. In the meantime, the staff of the *Tribune* was eagerly raking in rumors, off-the-record information, and it may be, bits of overheard conversation. On the 18th, under the bold heading, "THE MARY ROGERS MYSTERY EXPLAINED," it supplied the first full report:

> . . . this woman [Mrs. Loss] was accidentally wounded by the premature discharge of a gun in the hands of her son; the wound proved fatal; but before she died she sent for Justice Merritt of New Jersey, and told him the following facts. On the Sunday of Miss Rogers disappearance she came to her house from this city in company with a young physician who undertook to procure for her a premature delivery.—While in the hands of her physician she died and a consultation was then held as to the disposal of her body. It was finally taken at night by the son of Mrs. Loss and sunk in the river where it was found. Her clothes were first tied up in a bundle and sunk in a pond on the land of James G. King in that neighborhood; but it was afterwards thought they were not safe there, and they were accordingly taken and scattered through the woods as they were found.

The name of the physician is unknown to us, nor do we know whether it was divulged or not. The Mayor has been made acquainted with these facts by Mr. Merritt, and we doubt not an immediate inquiry after the guilty wretch will be made. The son of Mrs. Loss, as an accessory after the fact, we suppose will be, if he has not already been—arrested. No doubt, we apprehend, can be entertained of the truth of this confession. . . . Thus has this fearful mystery, which has struck fear and terror to so many hearts, been at last explained away by circumstances in which no one can fail to perceive a Providential agency. Besides the guilty murderer, the secret rested with two persons. One of these through the involuntary agency of the other, is laid upon her death-bed . . . .[7]

On the same day, the *Morning Courier,* more circumspect in its approach, gave a guarded paragraph of implications:

Murder of Mary C. Rogers.—Reports have been in circulation for some days past, that discoveries have been made as to the manner in which this unfortunate female came to her death. They rest on the following circumstances. On Saturday last we gave a report of an inquest which had been held by Justice Gilbert Merritt, of Hudson County, acting Coroner, on the body of Mrs. Frederica Loss, who has for some years past been keeper of the Nick Moore House, at the foot of Weehawken Hill, and who came to her death by the accidental discharge of a gun held in the hands of one of her sons. This woman—who, it will be recollected was examined at the time of finding the corpse, as to any information she might possess of the causes of the poor girl's death—it is said, before she died, charged her two sons to make known the circumstances attending the death of Mary Rogers, which she had before concealed. These two sons, we are informed, were yesterday arrested at Hackensack. We give these reports without vouching for their accuracy, although we are inclined to believe they are not without foundation.[8]

There can be no doubt that the death of Mrs. Loss *did* give rise to concrete revelations that connected the Loss family and their inn with the death of Mary Rogers, but, as Justice Merritt hastened to make clear, there had been no official interrogation and no confession *as such*. His denial appeared in the *Courier* on the 19th:

To Col. Webb:—

I noticed a statement in the Tribune of this morning, relative to a confession said to have been made before me by the late Mrs. Loss, which is entirely incorrect, as no such examination took place, nor could it, from the deranged state of Mrs. Loss' mind.

Respectfully Yours,

Gilbert Merritt

Hoboken, Nov. 18, 1842[9]

In making this statement, Merritt's position, it is clear, was a purely legal one; admissions of guilt from an apparently delirious woman would have no force. His affidavit of the 14th, however, charging Mrs. Loss and her sons with complicity, was sufficient to bring about an official hearing by Justice Lutkins, and this now took place on the 19th, at Jersey City. The three sons, some neighbors, and the family doctor were questioned, but nothing new or damaging was turned up. The "great secret" according to the testimony of one of the sons, was that "my mother would know when she died what became of the souls of the people who died"; according to another son the secret was merely a private cure for rheumatism. There was some discussion about a payment of $50 "offered by any one for any purpose," there were pointed questions about the clothes found in the thicket, and about the interior construction of the Loss inn, but the whole affair was tantalizingly inconclusive. At the finish of the hearing, however, Justice Lutkins and other magistrates remained in consultation with Mayor Morris of Hoboken, leading the *Herald* to conclude its coverage with: "It is understood there is something more of deep and overwhelming interest yet in the wind. The magistrates are on the scent and these investigations will not end here."[10] The *Morning Courier,* agreeing that the last word had not been spoken, commented: "This mysterious matter sleeps for the present."[11] Less coy than either of its New York colleagues, the *Newark Daily Advertiser,* which up to this point had been content to reprint coverage of the case from its big city rivals, stated explicitly: "The case of Mary Rogers remains, it seems, legally unexplained . . . . But we understand the investigation will be pursued, as it is believed that the recent statement of the manner of her death is probably true."[12]

At this juncture the facts concerning the death of Mrs. Loss end abruptly; nothing more seems to have come to light. But it was not the finish of the affair so far as the *Tribune* and the *Herald* were concerned. The *Tribune,* as a result of Merritt's disclaimer to the *Courier,* on November 21 retracted its assertion of an official confession, but insisted that the remainder of its story was substantially correct, reiterated its belief in a confession of some kind, and said that it had received its information from two New York City magistrates who were not named:

We gave the facts as they were told to us by two magistrates of this City, and as we understood them on the authority of a statement made by Mr. Merritt himself to Mayor Morris. We said nothing about any "examination" of Mrs. Loss and erred in stating that the *confession* was made to Mr. Merritt. That it was made to *someone* we have little doubt; and we firmly believe that the statement we give embraces the true explanation of the manner of this unfortunate woman's death.

On the same day the *Herald* took a swipe at its archrival by reprinting the *Tribune's* original story and Merritt's note of denial. On the following day the *Tribune* came back with a brief answer full of appropriate disdain: "Our envious neighbors who cannot endure the knowledge that we gave the first development of the Mary Rogers mystery, may as well forbear their snarling. They only set the public laughing at their ludicrous misery. That our first statement was substantially correct we are confident, and that we made it on good authority we know. Those who doubt can satisfy themselves by proper inquiries; those who can wait shall be publically satisfied."[13] But the *Herald,* possibly anticipating some such reply, on the same day demanded that the names of the two magistrates be revealed. The *Tribune* did not respond and on November 24th the *Herald* again insisted that the names be published. The *Tribune* continued to ignore all this and on November 26th reprinted in *The Weekly Tribune* the stories from the issues of the 18th and 21st.[14] Then, amid clouds of silence and confusion, the names of Frederica Loss and Mary Rogers faded from the category of contemporary news.

A contemporary sketch of
Mary Rogers, published in
the New York *Atlas,*
August 6, 1841

New York Public Library

CHAPTER FIVE

The language was ingeniously
framed . . . while in fact not a
shadow of meaning existed.

Poe, *Mystification*

Mystification

THE NEWS of the Weehawken developments, beginning on November 18, spread quickly. Poe, in Philadelphia, where the papers regularly copied New York items, must have known of it almost immediately either through his own reading or by having it called to his attention. Certainly Snowden himself, or someone else from the *Companion,* which was about to publish the final instalment of *Marie Roget,* would have contacted him. Perhaps by November 20, then, or surely within a few days thereafter, Poe possessed all available information regarding the death of Mrs. Loss and the inconclusive Lutkins hearing. The knowledge would have come as a disaster: despite the absence of proof, it all added up to the strong probability that Mary Rogers had died in an abortion attempt and had not been throttled, as Poe's story concluded, by a naval officer or any other individual.

He was at this time in a particularly depressed period: he was still struggling with poverty, as well as worry over his wife's health, and had resumed his drinking and his erratic habits. A visitor to his home in Wistar Lane (now Brandywine Alley) in September 1842, only some three weeks before the news of Mrs. Loss's death reached

61

the public, has left a revealing picture:

> He lived in a rural home on the outskirts of the city. His house was small,
> but comfortable inside for one of the kind. The rooms looked neat and
> orderly, but everything about the place wore an air of pecuniary want.
> Although I arrived late in the morning Mrs. Clemm, Poe's mother-in-law,
> was busy preparing for his breakfast. My presence possibly caused some
> confusion, but I noticed there was delay and evident difficulty in procuring
> the meal. His wife entertained me. Her manners were agreeable and
> graceful. She had well-formed, regular features, with the most expressive
> and intelligent eyes I have ever beheld. Her pale complexion, the deep
> lines in her face and a consumptive cough made me regard her as the
> victim for an early grave. She and her mother showed much concern about
> Eddie, as they called Poe, and were anxious to have him secure work. . . .
> When Poe appeared his dark hair hung carelessly over his high forehead,
> and his dress was a little slovenly. He met me cordially, but was reserved,
> and complained of feeling unwell. His pathetic tenderness and loving
> manners towards his wife impressed me. I was not long in observing with
> deep regret that he had fallen again into habits of intemperance. . . . We
> visited the city together and had an engagement for the following day. I
> left him sober, but he did not keep the engagement and wrote me that he
> was ill.[1]

In such an evidently unsteady condition of mind and body, Poe's
agitation over the Loss revelations, with their direct threat to his
reputation, must have been extreme. His hopes for the launching of
his own magazine were high and he may have already begun
discussions with Thomas C. Clarke for the financing of it. By
October he had declined an offer to return as editor of *Graham's
Magazine*, perhaps indicating that he had even then received
assurances that his dream would become a reality.[2] In the
circumstances, it would have been surprising had he not attempted
to extricate himself from the impending embarrassment of the final
instalment of *Marie Roget*.

As an experienced magazine editor, he undoubtedly considered
the feasibility of omitting the final instalment of the story from the
January *Companion*, but that idea he must have promptly rejected
since it would have been an admission of abject failure. Much
better, obviously, would be a use of the dramatic developments at
Weehawken to heighten the story's effect—some slight calculation
would have told him there were still a few days before the January
issue would go on the presses.[3] He could not revamp the story

entirely because his "naval officer" had appeared at the end of the
second instalment, but nerves much duller than Poe's would have
been required to avoid doing *something* in such a situation. A letter
was not the answer since there was insufficient time for an exchange
of correspondence that would, of necessity, have been highly
complicated. The only logical alternative is that sometime in late
November Poe took the six-hour train ride to New York, where he
persuaded Snowden to postpone the third segment of *Marie Roget* to
the February issue so that changes could be made in it.[4] His presence
in New York is almost demanded by the situation: he would scarcely
have attempted to make revisions solely on the strength of the
excited newspaper reports that had reached him up to November 20
since, for all he knew, fresh revelations might come at any time. He
needed to know how matters stood behind the headlines.

So far this is conjecture—legitimate enough, but still conjecture.
There are two incidents in Poe biography, however, which tend to
support the hypothesis of a visit to New York about this time. The
first is the well-known interlude described in "Poe's Mary," a
magazine article which in the past has been looked on with a
certain amount of distrust.

"Mary" first appeared in *Harper's Monthly* in 1889.[5] Written by
one Augustus Van Cleef, the article identifies neither Mary nor the
author, except that Van Cleef mentions he is a relative of Mary's.
The narrative purports to be the reminiscences of an old Baltimore
sweetheart of Poe's, told largely in her own words. The pertinent
portion of the article is the account Mary gives of an unexpected
visit she received from Poe one day in 1842 while she was living in
Jersey City. Mary placed the incident in the spring of 1842, but Van
Cleef himself doubts the old lady's precision as to dates, and it is
quite possible that the visit took place in November of that year. In
the framework of Poe biography, as it is presently accepted, this trip
to New Jersey has never made a great deal of sense, usually
presenting itself as a perplexing aberration. Taken in relation to the
suddenly pressing situation surrounding *Marie Roget,* however, it
assumes some real significance.

According to her story, Mary had enjoyed the youthful Poe's
attentions in Baltimore, probably in 1832, had met him later in
Philadelphia, in 1840-41, but had lost contact thereafter. With her

husband she had moved first to New York, then across the river to
Jersey City. It was here that Poe briefly, if disconcertingly, reentered
her life.

> When living in Jersey City, I saw Mr. Poe again. He was still living in
> Philadelphia. He came to New York and went to my husband's place of
> business to find out where we lived. He was on a spree however, and forgot
> the address. He made several trips backward and forward on the ferryboat.
> He asked different people on board if they knew where I lived, and finally
> found a deck-hand, who happened to know, and told him. Mr. Poe said he
> was determined to find me, if he "had to go to hell" to do it. When my
> husband returned home he was told on the boat that a crazy man had been
> looking for his wife!
>
> When Mr. Poe reached our house I was out with my sister, and he opened
> the door for us when we got back. We saw he was on one of his sprees, and
> he had been away from home for several days. He said to me: "So you have
> married that cursed——(referring to her husband's business). Do you love
> him truly? Did you marry him for love?" I answered "That's nobody's
> business; that is between my husband and myself." He then said: "You
> don't love him. You do love me. You know you do."
>
> Mr. Poe staid to tea with us, but ate nothing; only drank a cup of tea. He
> got excited in conversation and taking up a table-knife, began to chop at
> some radishes in a dish in front of him. He cut them all up and the pieces
> flew over the table, to everybody's amusement. After tea he asked me if I
> would not play and sing for him, and I sang his favorite song again. He
> then went away. A few days afterward Mrs. Clemm came to see me, much
> worried about "Eddie dear" as she always addressed him. She did not know
> where he was and his wife was almost crazy with anxiety. I told Mrs.
> Clemm that he had been to see me. A search was made and he was finally
> found in the woods on the outskirts of Jersey City, wandering about like a
> crazy man. Mrs. Clemm took him back with her to Philadelphia.

The picture may have been out of focus in some of its details
when Mary recalled it after so many years, but its basic facts ring
true: sometime in 1842 Poe, agitated and under pressure, was in
New York and New Jersey—was, as a matter of fact, within only a
few minutes of Hoboken and Weehawken. It is not indicated
precisely where on the outskirts of Jersey City he was found by Mrs.
Clemm and the other searchers, but if it was to the north, then his
presence in Hoboken is established, putting him within a short walk
of the neighborhood of the Loss inn.

A second sudden and unexplained appearance in New York about
this time, which also carries a note of strangeness, is that recorded by
Gabriel Harrison, sometime actor-storekeeper and friend of the

literary. Recalling his first meeting with Poe, at his store for "general merchandise" located at the corner of Broadway and Prince Street, Harrison says he did not know who Poe was, but invited him in because he had been staring wistfully at the cigars in the window. Poe, Harrison stated further, did not reveal his identity, but gave his name as "Thaddeus K. Peasley." It was not until a later visit, when Fitz-Green Halleck happened to be present in the store and recognized Poe, that Harrison discovered who his visitor really was. The date of the first meeting Harrison remembered as early 1843, but it could well have been late 1842.[6]

There is thus some biographical support for the supposition that Poe went to New York in November-December 1842—and no known fact disputes it. But what evidence is there for the hypothesis that he made changes in *Marie Roget* before publication? To begin with, there is the basic and extremely relevant fact that the final instalment of the story was postponed, without any explanation or evident necessity, from January to February. It must have been that Poe could not satisfy himself about the Loss revelations in time to make changes for the January issue, which would have been locked up by early December. Even with the postponement, obviously, the situation remained urgent. If he arrived in New York in late November, spent a few days or a week making inquiries in the city, and tapping whatever sources were available to him on the other side of the river, he could not have had much more than another few days to make his changes. In any case, it is known that he was back in Philadelphia on Christmas Day.[7]

In the absence of Poe's original manuscript it is not possible, of course, to say with absolute certainty just what changes were made at this time, but the text reveals some interesting internal evidence. Since it is unlikely that Poe's personal investigations could have turned up much of importance beyond what had already appeared in the papers, it is evident that any changes would have been e_uivocal or temporizing ones. Now, in fact, there are *two* points in the final instalment of *Marie Roget,* as it appeared in the *Companion,* where equivocation gleams fitfully through a tangle of verbiage grossly untypical of the usual Poe clarity. And both points touch directly upon the subject of the Loss revelations. Each of these probably conceals a revision.

The first occurs in the passage in which Poe is discussing the
Weehawken thicket as the scene of the crime.[8] A peculiar hesitation
or vacillation is very evident:

> Notwithstanding the acclamation with which the discovery of this thicket
> was received by the press, and the unanimity with which it was supposed to
> indicate the precise scene of the outrage, it must be admitted that there
> was some very good reason for doubt. That it *was* the scene, I believe—but
> there was excellent reason for doubt . . . .

After a lengthy and minute presentation of arguments against the
thicket, with supreme illogic he is still able to say: "You will not
have apprehended me rightly, however, if you suppose it is my
design to deny this thicket as the scene of the outrage . . . ." The
uncertainty is clear. But the entire section betrays an effort to
incorporate a line of reasoning *against* the thicket as the scene of the
crime, with another line of reasoning that proceeds *from* the
evidence of the thicket to disprove a gang theory. The attempted
amalgamation is not successful, and there is an unmistakably
jumbled air pervading the passage. Indeed, no attempt of the sort
could have succeeded, since the two lines of reasoning are directly
contrary.[9] What appears to have occurred is this: he originally
denied the thicket as the scene of the crime *by a gang*, asserting that
it could only have been the scene involving *one individual*. Then,
during the hurried revision he perceived happily that a portion of
his denial fitted well with the new situation, so he tried to expand
on it.

The second change is the quite palpable tacking-on of the two
paragraphs with which the story ends. In these superfluous passages
Poe laboriously warns the reader against any detailed comparison of
the fates of *Marie Roget* and Mary Rogers. They are repetitious,
obtuse and badly written. Their whole intent is to forestall any too-
serious linking of the story with the Rogers case—while the *opening*
of the story, in the November issue, blatantly *invited* such
comparison. The probability—perhaps the near-certainty—is that
Marie Roget originally concluded at the sentence: "With God all is
Now." The next paragraph, significantly, opens with the words, "I
repeat, then . . . ."

These changes, as well as others which are impossible now to
trace, were makeshift, but they were undoubtedly the best that Poe

could manage in the limited time available and in the grip of the unsettled situation. At least they saved him—and Dupin—from outright failure. Sometime during the middle of December a more relaxed Poe (and a relieved Mrs. Clemm?) boarded the train for the return to Philadelphia. Behind him, Poe may have thought he had at last set to rest the ghost of the Beautiful Cigar Girl. In reality, her career had only just begun.

There does not seem to have been any marked contemporary reaction to the final instalment of *Marie Roget*. Like most magazine fiction, of that day as well as this, it quickly faded from public attention.

In Philadelphia during the ensuing year, Poe's fortunes did not improve, and by April of 1844, accompanied by his family, he was on his way back to New York with the evident intention of making it his permanent home. His "Balloon Hoax" was published soon after his arrival, "The Raven" was probably under way at this time, and the Chevalier C. Auguste Dupin—recovered from his close shave in the *Roget* case—had begun looking into a delicate matter of a purloined letter, but little else of moment seems to have taken place during these months, except the desultory *Letters from Gotham* contributed to the Columbia *Spy* in Pennsylvania. In one of these, he refers briefly to the Mary Rogers case, citing it as an instance of inept police work, but his comments seem to arise more from annoyance that his story had misfired and failed to attract any attention.[10] By October, severe financial strain compelled him to look for steady work, and he found it at the offices of the *Evening Mirror,* then located, of all places, at the corner of Nassau and Ann streets, only a few doors from Mary Rogers' old home. Here, for the next four or five months, Poe came daily to act as assistant editor and critic. It thus happened that when the necessity for further revising *The Mystery of Marie Roget* arose early in 1845 Poe found himself ideally situated for another and more thorough review of the behind-the-scenes status of the real case. His circle of contacts in New York, if occasionally strained, was wide; one likely channel for inside information would be Richard Adams Locke, who had been prominent in the citizens' meeting at the Stoneall house, and who had bought Poe's balloon story for the *Sun* in April 1844.

The need for revision arose as a result of the huge success of "The Raven." The poem was published on January 29, 1845, and the resulting fame of the mournful black bird threw wide the doors to opportunity. Poe was invited to join the staff of the *Broadway Journal,* with a share in its profits; the Rutgers Female Institute, on Madison Street near Clinton, asked him to judge the compositions of its young ladies; fashionable New York went to hear him lecture on the poets and poetry of America; the Literati, just beginning to become a brilliant company, invited him into their salons; and the publishers Wiley and Putnam arranged to bring out "The Raven" and his other poems, as well as a volume of short stories.[11]

Tales was published by Wiley and Putnam in June 1845. It contained twelve pieces and was heavily weighted toward the analytical, a situation that irked Poe, since he felt that the book should have reflected the varied nature of his writings. It is not known precisely when the publisher agreed to take the volume, but it was most probably in February, when excitement over "The Raven" was at its height. Preparation of the manuscript for *Tales* did not require much work on Poe's part since eight of the stories had already been revised as part of the projected *Phantasy Pieces,* which he had unsuccessfully offered to Harper's in September of 1844.[12] The inclusion of *Marie Roget* in *Tales* was due to the presence of Dupin, since, judged on its own, it had little of the cohesion and finish that distinguished its two companion pieces; also it had been mentioned along with the *Rue Morgue* in the opening paragraph of *The Purloined Letter.* In any case the story still had some contemporary value, enhanced perhaps by the publication in

Cover of an 1844 novel
loosely based on
the Mary Rogers case

PRICE, 12 CENTS.

THE

BEAUTIFUL CIGAR GIRL;

OR,

The Mysteries of Broadway.

BY

J. H. INGRAHAM, Esq.,

1844 of a potboiling novel entitled *The Beautiful Cigar Girl,*
written by J. H. Ingraham.[13]

What Poe proceeded to do now deserves some measure of
admiration—even if grudgingly given—for its nonchalant audacity.
He made fifteen small, almost undetectable changes in the story, all
of which definitely accommodate the possibility of an abortion death
at the inn of Madame Deluc (his fictional name for Mrs. Loss)—and
then he added detailed footnotes so that it would appear he had
been entirely correct from the start! The significance of these later
changes was first discovered by William Kurtz Wimsatt,[14] who
reported them with rather too much of scholarly detachment in
1941—thus making *Marie Roget,* when judged on the score of
durability, certainly Poe's greatest hoax.

First the deletions.[15] Following are the three passages from which
Poe dropped significant material; the words he deleted are printed
in boldface.

1

You will here bear in mind that **I admit the thicket as the scene of the
outrage; and you will immediately perceive that** the arguments urged
against the thicket . . . .[16]

2

The circumstances of the first elopement, as mentioned by Le Mercurie,
tend to blend the idea of this seaman with that of the 'naval officer' who is
first known to have led the unfortunate into crime. **We are not forced to
suppose a premeditated design of murder or of violation. But there was the
friendly shelter of the thicket, and the approach of rain—there was
opportunity and strong temptation—and then a sudden and violent wrong,
to be concealed only by one of darker dye.**[17]

3

For reasons which we shall not specify but which to many readers will
appear obvious, we have taken the liberty of here omitting, from the MSS.
placed in our hands, such portions as details the following up of the
apparently slight clew obtained by Dupin. We feel it advisable only to
state, in brief, that the result desired was brought to pass; **that an
individual assassin was convicted, upon his own confession, of the murder
of Marie Roget,** and that the Prefect fulfilled punctually, although with
reluctance, the terms of his compact with the Chevalier.[18]

Thus he rid the narrative of an absolute commitment to murder
by one man in the Weehawken thicket. Now it remained for him to
insinuate the possibility of an abortion death at the Loss inn (the

Deluc inn, of course, in the story)—no easy task in such a complex and closely reasoned context, especially when the emendations had to be unnoticeable. Here are the twelve ingenious additions.

1

That she did meet with some companion, and proceed with him across the river, reaching the Barrière du Roule at so late an hour as three o'clock in the afternoon, is known. But in consenting so to accompany this individual, **(for whatever purpose—to her mother known or unknown,)** she must have thought . . . .[19]

2

We may imagine her thinking thus—'I am to meet a certain person for the purpose of elopement, **or for certain other purposes known only to myself.'**[20]

3

But as it is my design never to return—**or not for some weeks—or not until certain concealments are effected—**[21]

4

Notwithstanding the acclamation with which the discovery of this thicket was received by the press, and the unanimity with which it was supposed to indicate the precise scene of the outrage, it must be admitted that there was some very good reason for doubt. That it was the scene, **I may or I may not** believe—but there was excellent reason for doubt.[22]

5

You will not have apprehended me rightly, however, if you suppose it my design to deny this thicket as the scene of the outrage. **There might have been a wrong here, or, more possibly, an accident at Madame Deluc's.**[23]

6

We will resume this question by mere allusion to the revolting details of the surgeon examined at the inquest. It is only necessary to say that his published inferences, in regard to the number of the ruffians, have been properly ridiculed as unjust and totally baseless, by all the reputable anatomists of Paris. Not that the matter might not have been as inferred, but that there was no ground for the inference—**was there not much for another?**[24]

7

The solitary murderer, having borne the corpse for some distance, **(whether from the thicket or elsewhere)** by means of the bandage hitched around its middle . . . .[25]

8

. . . that is to say, arising, as we have imagined, after quitting the thicket **(if the thicket it was),** and on the road between the thicket and the river.[26]

9

But the gang which has drawn upon itself the pointed animadversion, although the somewhat tardy **and very suspicious** evidence of Madame Deluc, is the only gang which is represented . . . .[27]

10

The horrors of this dark deed are known only to one, **or two,** living human beings, and to God.[28]

11

Let us sum up the meagre yet certain fruits of our long analysis. We have attained the idea **either of a fatal accident under the roof of Madame Deluc, or** of a murder perpetrated in the thicket . . . .[29]

12

Let us endeavor to ascertain, by repeated questionings of Madame Deluc and her boys, as well as of the omnibus-driver, Valence, something more of the personal appearance and bearing of the 'man of dark complexion.' Queries, skillfully directed, will not fail to elicit, from some of these parties, information on this particular point **(or upon others)** . . . .[30]

The changes involve only some 150 words—infinitesimal in comparison with the 20,000-word story—yet the care and skill with which they were made—despite perhaps the most intense scrutiny ever afforded the life and works of an American writer—concealed for nearly a century the masquerade of the Parisian *grisette*.

Just what perverse imp prompted Poe to go beyond these textual changes and supply the attention-getting footnotes, it is difficult to say; certainly, though, the boldness of the action adds an air of confidence to the claim that he had succeeded in solving the mystery. There are twenty-four notes in all, mostly identifying the sources of the various newspaper extracts, the originals of the characters and the New York counterparts of the Parisian locations.[31] It is only the first note, however, that is of real interest. Here it is in its entirety, as it appeared in the *Tales* of 1845 and as it has been reprinted ever since:

> Upon the original publication of "Marie Roget," the foot-notes now appended were considered unnecessary; but the lapse of several years since the tragedy upon which the tale is based, renders it expedient to give them, and also to say a few words in explanation of the general design. A young girl, *Mary Cecilia Rogers* was murdered in the vicinity of New York;

and although her death occasioned an intense and long-enduring
excitement, the mystery attending it had remained unsolved at the period
when the present paper was written and published (November 1842).
Herein, under pretense of relating the fate of a Parisian grisette, the
author has followed, in minute detail, the essential, while merely
paralleling the inessential, facts of the real murder of Mary Rogers. Thus
all argument founded upon the fiction is applicable to the truth: and the
investigation of the truth was the object.

   The "Mystery of Marie Roget" was composed at a distance from the scene
of the atrocity, and with no other means of investigation than the
newspapers afforded. Thus, much escaped the writer of which he could
have availed himself had he been upon the spot and visited the localities.
It may not be improper to record, nevertheless, that the confessions of *two*
persons (one of them the Madame Deluc of the narrative), made at
different periods, long subsequent to the publication, confirmed, in full,
not only the general conclusion, but absolutely *all* the chief hypothetical
details by which that conclusion was attained.

Those words, for one reader, at least, always call up a picture of
Poe chuckling over the manuscript of the revised *Marie Roget,*
much in the manner he himself described in "Diddling Considered
as One of the Exact Sciences": "Your true diddler winds up all with
a grin. . . . He goes home. He locks his door. He divests himself of
his clothes. He puts out his candle. He gets into bed. He places his
head upon the pillow. All this done, and your diddler grins." If Poe
ever grinned in his life he must have done so when he finished
composing that note. The general falsehood of the claim is obvious,
but there are a number of virtuoso touches. The story was written
in April-May 1842, not November 1842. The "confession" of
Madame Deluc was the revelation of the dying Mrs. Loss, of course,
but it was made while the story was running serially, not "long
subsequent to publication." It was true that the story had been
composed "at a distance from the scene of the tragedy," but the
distance could easily have been covered in under six hours. In fact,
aside from the probability that he went to New York in November
of 1842, shortly after completion of the tale he *did* make the trip
from Philadelphia to New York and was therefore "upon the spot"
and could comfortably have "visited the localities." And the only
thing "confirmed" was Poe's ability to land on his feet.[32]

   His reference to a supposed second confession may be nothing
more than further "mystification," but, just possibly, it may reflect

inside knowledge, gained perhaps in some newspaper office along Nassau Street, of information supplied by one of the Loss boys subsequent to the Lutkins hearing. It is this possibility that remains the one intriguing element in Poe's story: was there some kind of a deal—immunity for accomplices in exchange for a confession—and is this perhaps the reason why nothing further has ever come to light?[33] It may also be taken as a strong possibility that Mary's mother was aware of all the facts and divulged them under pressure; it is not likely that she was unaware of her daughter's pregnancy. A final point regarding the "confession of Madame Deluc" should not be overlooked: when Poe published the footnote in the *Tales* of 1845, there were many persons in the city who remembered the case, many police officers and reporters who had been closely associated with the investigation. Poe must have been very sure of his information to bring it so unequivocally before these people. And as late as 1848 he still accepted the abortion theory, as is shown by a reference in one of his letters to George Eveleth.[34]

The footnote did its work well.[35] It fooled Rufus Griswold, who alludes favorably to it in the *Memoir* of 1850, and it was accepted by Poe's first formal biographer, W. F. Gill, who quotes the portion in which Poe claimed success. By the turn of the century it had established itself, and the legend, so firmly that it gave rise to such entirely gratuitous assertions as: "There was a story current, impossible now to verify, that fifteen or twenty years afterwards, a sailor, dying in a hospital, confessed to the murder, giving details which substantially agreed with Poe's narrative."[36] By 1963 it had even worked its way into serious criticism: D. E. S. Maxwell, in *American Fiction*, comments: "Poe reasons out a common and sordid city murder, a girl strangled and mutilated. The enduring interest of the story is not that in it Poe edged his way towards the solution of an actual crime, remarkable though that is. What gives the story its substance is the nature of the crime, and Poe's presentation of it. It becomes a parable in the violent elisions in the fragile security of social life . . . ."[37] Of course it was nothing of the sort. In the light of what has been demonstrated in these pages, *The Mystery of Marie Roget* must be counted, finally, as nothing more or less than a classic performance in the annals of literary hugger-mugger.

EPILOGUE

Some Loose Ends

During the twenty-five years following Poe's death in 1849, Mary Rogers and *Marie Roget* were both largely forgotten. In 1851 Mary's death found place in one of the phony "confession" pamphlets that abounded at the time,[1] and in 1869 it was used as the basis of an incident in an obscure novel, *Tales of a Physician,* by Andrew J. Davis,[2] but these were ephemeral things. Of itself the case lacked any of the bizarre or unusual features that keep such tragedies alive. It was only in *The Mystery of Marie Roget,* and its footnotes, that the girl's fate retained any vitality, but it was not until some thirty-five years after Poe had made his furtive changes that the factual background of the narrative received any pointed comment. This occurred in the first full-scale biography, by John Ingram, and over the next six or seven years the Mary Rogers case was prominently treated in three different true-crime collections, establishing it among the minor classics of the genre. But along with this unlooked-for revival of the forty-year-old case, Ingram unwittingly provided a little mystery of his own to garnish subsequent discussion. "The naval officer implicated," he unexpectedly remarked, "was named Spencer."[3]

He said nothing else, just dropped that one name into his text, without comment, elaboration, or indication as to source—but so quirky are the vicissitudes of literature that not one of the nine writers who treated the theme in the sixty years after Ingram took up the thread. Winthrop Lane, writing for *Collier's Magazine* in 1930, went so far as to visit the New Jersey sites of the tragedy, and search the basement of the Hudson County Courthouse in an unsuccessful hunt for the records of the original inquest on Mary's body, but he entirely ignored Ingram's "Spencer."[4] It was not until 1941 that any writer attempted to deal with Ingram's laconic statement; this was the effort by William K. Wimsatt Jr. to approach the case in a serious and scholarly manner. With regard to Spencer, he simply checked the printed records of U.S. naval officers and consulted the naval archives at Washington, D.C. This action was legitimate enough in itself, but it serves to highlight the giddiness that afflicts all who traffic with *Marie Roget,* since Wimsatt had already in his article amply demonstrated that *no* naval officer, nor any other individual killer, was implicated in Mary's death. But, perhaps carried away by his headlong pursuit of Poe's twistings and turnings, he plunged on, with the following result:

> Without corroboration from some other quarter this statement of Ingram's proves of course nothing. But it may not be irrelevant to add that there *was* one naval officer—and only one—named Spencer who could have been "implicated." In the summer of 1841 there were two U.S. naval officers named Spencer, but one of these was in Ohio. The other, a native of New York and resident by turns of West Farms (part of the present Bronx) and of New York City, a man forty-eight years old in 1841, was "on leave" during 1837 and 1838 and "waiting orders" during 1840 and 1841. In his correspondence with the Navy Department he complains of a chronic infirmity and asks continually to be excused, but in December, 1841, he asks to be assigned a command. He resigns from the navy in December, 1843. This was Captain William A. Spencer (1793-1854); his brother was J. C. Spencer (1788-1855), Secretary of War in 1841-1843; and their father was Judge Ambrose Spencer (1765-1848), an important figure in New York politics. Enough of scandal was the lot of this family when in December, 1842, Philip Spencer, a wild young midshipman, son of the Secretary of War, was hanged at sea for attempting mutiny on board the brig *Somers.*[5]

Having dredged up a Spencer, one, moreover, of "influential family," Wimsatt let it go at that, but in a passing comment on the

unfortunate Philip Spencer of the *Somers,* he says "The case was
widely discussed. It seems not impossible that the notoriety of Philip
Spencer (who became midshipman in November, 1841) may
somehow have produced Ingram's statement." Thus, after quite
deflating Poe's one excursion into real-life crime, Wimsatt
concluded his article by undoing a good part of his work and
leaving readers with the uneasy feeling that all had not yet been said
on the matter. And indeed it hadn't, or so it seemed, for a little
more than a decade after Wimsatt's article appeared, young Philip
Spencer himself stood charged with Mary's murder. Irving Wallace,
in his *The Fabulous Originals,* a treatment of sundry literary
characters and their real-life models which came out in 1955, in
concluding his chapter on Mary Rogers, by-passed Wimsatt's middle-
aged Spencer, and fastened on Philip. He was, Wallace thought, "a
definite and fascinating possibility."[6]

At this point the lines become so tangled that it is difficult to
trace them, and, it must be admitted, the effort at times hardly
seems worthwhile. To begin with, the idea of a "naval officer,"
supposedly introduced into the case by Poe, had never been a real
possibility. The police had grasped this clue as one of its first leads,
as the repeated questioning of Kiekuck shows, and if there had been
any naval officer involved in Mary's 1838 disappearance, he would
very early have been found and questioned. The paragraph in the
Herald, in which he makes his first appearance, had been printed for
the very purpose of calling public attention to such a possibility, and
the story specified, it should be remembered, that "his name is well
known on board his ship." Poe's use of the naval officer in the first
version of his story, depended on an intimate connection with Mary's
first disappearance, but this whole idea evaporated in the second
version, which Poe doctored to allow for death by abortion. Even if
there were—which there was not—some naval officer connected with
Mary in both 1838 and 1841, Philip Spencer could not have been the
one: in the fall of 1838 he was a fifteen-year-old student at Geneva
College, Schenectady, New York.[7]

What about Captain William Spencer? Since it is morally certain
that Mary's death occurred on an abortion table, the concept of a
naval officer has no validity, except as it is a euphemism for
"abortionist." The fact that the unsuspecting Captain William

Spencer was in New York both in 1838 and 1841 isn't really
enough, after all, to make him a suspect. The sort of free-wheeling
speculation this represents could, if it tried, find other outlets: there
are, for example, over a dozen Spencers lurking in the New York
City directories for 1838 and a like number for 1841. Not only that,
but a comparison reveals that *seven* of them had left the city by
1842! None, disappointingly, were doctors.

Wimsatt, however, may have been closer to truth in one
hypothesis: the notoriety of Philip Spencer's execution may have
somehow induced Poe to name him willy-nilly, as implicated with
Mary, perhaps as the father of her unborn child (remembering, of
course, that it was not necessary to have a "naval officer" in the first
place, and that Philip Spencer was not an officer in either 1838 or
1841). Spencer was hanged at sea on December 1, 1842. The brig
Somers reached New York on the 14th, and on December 17th the
news reached the public, causing great excitement.[8] If the theory of
Poe's hurried trip to New York in late November 1842, in order to
make changes in his story, is correct, then he was probably still in
the city when the news about Spencer first broke. In any event, the
case quickly received nationwide attention that lasted for three
months, and Philip Spencer in all of this was portrayed as a very
dissipated young man. Sometime shortly before Poe's death,
probably in 1848, he told Mrs. Helen Whitman that the "naval
officer" of his story was named "Spencer." Just what he told her
beyond that, or if he indicated exactly who this Spencer was, is not
known. Mrs. Whitman in March 1867 passed the information on to
the inquisitive George Eveleth, and a copy of her letter was
supplied to Ingram in 1878 for use in the biography; thus the still-
veiled "Spencer" found his way into the story of Mary Rogers.[9]

More rewarding speculation is afforded by a glance at the
subsequent career of Mary's original employer and sponsor, John
Anderson. Despite the fact that Mary's soubriquet tied her rather
closely to Anderson and his store, he played no prominent part in
the investigations, and, apart from a listing among contributors to
the reward money, his name is scarcely mentioned in the news
columns. Afterwards, he continued in New York as a tobacconist,
and soon began to prosper. He marketed his own brand of chewing
tobacco, Anderson's Solace Tobacco, a name derived from a

complimentary remark made in his store by General Winfield Scott, and shipped large quantities of it to the American army fighting in Mexico. The Gold Rush, soon afterwards, carried his name and his tobacco across the continent, where the forty-niners used prodigious amounts of it. (The secret seems to have been in the packaging: Anderson was one of the first to preserve a product's freshness by wrapping it in tinfoil.)

In 1850 he was one of a group of businessmen which tried, unsuccessfully, to establish a "railroad" (trolley line) on Broadway. He also exercised his abilities on New York real estate, and this, with other ventures, in time made him a millionaire and a man well known in social and political circles. About 1875 he bought an imposing manor in Tarrytown, New York, had the windows of the large house fitted with steel shutters, and settled down for good. In 1880 he tried to found a newspaper as an organ for the Democrats, but it failed within a year and he lost thousands on the attempt. He died in Paris on November 22, 1881, leaving everything to his eldest son, Charles, for some reason effectively disinheriting his other five children. Predictably, the will was contested and during the next decade the New York courts were seldom without litigation growing out of the Anderson will. The testimony elicited during some of the questioning in these cases, assuming some degree of truth in it, throws the last faint gleam of light on the fate of Mary Rogers.[10]

Her ghost, it appears, bedeviled Anderson nearly as much as it did Poe, and in more ways than one; it seems to have interfered, for example, with his political ambitions. One witness, an acquaintance, testified that while he and Anderson were passing near Mary's house one day, the tobacconist suddenly and vehemently damned the place as "the cause of driving him out of politics and belittling him in New York and which had kept him from advancing." That scene could have taken place no later than 1852, since the house at 126 Nassau was taken down that year,[11] but the ill fame of the dead girl continued to pursue him. Sometime after the Civil War, it is said, Fernando Wood tried to interest Anderson in running for mayor of New York, but, still wary of the notoriety that might result, he refused.

Just why Mary's death should have affected him to such an extent is not clear. The only possibility that presents itself, interestingly enough, is connected with James Gordon Bennett and the *Herald*. According to Anderson's own words, as related by a witness under oath in 1891, he had been more intimately connected with the investigation of Mary's death than had appeared at the time: he had been arrested on suspicion, or at least held for questioning, and subsequently discharged for lack of evidence. This action, Anderson claimed, had become known to Bennett, "and the suspicion cast upon him had injured his reputation and seriously interfered with his political prospects." The injury and the interference, if done at all, must have been by rumor and innuendo in the inner circles of the city's ruling factions, but there is some corroboration in the columns of the *Herald* itself. On August 3, 1841, in a roundup of information, the paper boldly stated that Mary had "three years ago lived with Anderson, the cigar man," and it revealed a settled prejudice, justified or not, against the man and his store when it remarked "she has not been at Anderson's hole for nearly three years." Such public comment, obviously, points to the probability of more vociferous denunciation in private. The reason for this journalistic bitterness can perhaps be seen in another admission of Anderson's, related by another witness in 1891—an admission that brings the manner of Mary's death suddenly closer to reality, as a part of the whole pattern of her life. Anderson, according to the witness, admitted that "an abortion had been committed on the girl—the year before her murder took place, or a year and a half—something of that kind—and that he got into some trouble about it—and outside of that there was no grounds on earth for anybody to suppose he had anything to do with the murder." But he himself, Anderson insisted, had had nothing to do, directly, with the abortion, thus creating an impression that he may have been admitting complicity as a fixer, or arranger.[12]

Beyond all that, Mary's ghost, in a more tangible way, continued to hover in Anderson's vicinity. As unlikely as it seems, the shrewd man of business became involved with spiritualism, and was persuaded that Mary occasionally appeared to him, moving and speaking, advising him on investments and even discussing the circumstances of her death and naming her killers. This was declared by more than one witness, especially by Anderson's close friend Abner Mattoon, former state senator and leading citizen of

Oswego, New York, who on two different occasions, in 1885 and 1891, made reference to it under oath. This aspect of Anderson's interests, however, comes to the present at too many removes from its beginnings, and no further details are available. It was, in the first place, introduced as evidence of Anderson's mental incompetence, but seems to have failed of its purpose. The Anderson litigation also provided what might be considered the final twist in the long and tortuous trail laid down by *The Mystery of Marie Roget*. At one point, for some unknown reason, the notion arose that Anderson had paid Poe to write the story in order to divert suspicion from himself.[13] And that, assuredly, is the proper moment at which to bid a final farewell to The Beautiful Cigar Girl and her Parisian counterpart.

Notes

CHAPTER ONE—MURDER IN OLD NEW YORK

1. It has become something of a fashion to play down Poe's primary role in the history of detective fiction. Without entering too deeply into the topic, it cannot really be denied that while stories with detective elements existed before Poe created Dupin, it was only with Poe that these elements, especially the idea of analysis and deduction from observed fact, were crystallized into a recognizable, repeatable technique. Only with Poe did the detective assume the central role. A clear demonstration of this can be found in *The Development of the Detective Novel* by A. E. Murch (London, 1958).

2. Irving Wallace, *The Fabulous Originals* (1955), pp. 214-15.

3. Hervey Allen, *Israfel* (1934), p. 409.

4. Frances Winwar, *The Haunted Palace* (1959), pp. 226-27.

5. Arthur H. Quinn, *Edgar Allan Poe. A Critical Biography* (1941), pp. 355-58.

6. J. W. Ostrom, ed., *The Letters of Edgar Allan Poe,* I, pp. 199-200. The italics are Poe's.

7. A. E. Murch, *The Development of the Detective Novel,* p. 73.

8. See, for instance, New York *Commercial Advertiser,* October 11, 1838, a story headed "More Traffic in Dead Bodies."

9. New York *Daily Express,* August 4, 1841, p. 1, col. 4.

10. New York *Atlas,* August 8, 1841, p. 1.

11. New York *Tribune,* August 26, 1841.

12. *Tribune,* August 19, 1841.

13. At No. 321, not 319 as some of the literature on the case will have it; see city directories. Also, contemporary mention places Anderson's store at the "City Hospital" on Broadway, which included No. 321. The New York *Business Directory* for 1838, I should warn the reader, is no help at all; under "Importers—Segars" it lists Anderson at 2 Wall Street, and gives, as the only tobacconist on Broadway, McDonald and Laird at 312.

14. "The Beautiful Cigar Girl," by McDonald Clarke, New York *Herald,* September 21, 1841. The poem consists of twenty limping quatrains on the evils of lust and liquor.

15. An explanation for this unsupported legend may be the following: The verses to Mary, by McDonald Clarke, just quoted, appeared in the *Herald* on September 21. In the same paper, on September 24, in almost the same position on page 1, there was printed an old poem of Halleck's in which he apostrophized the view from Weehawken Hill ("Weehawken! in thy mountain scenery . . ."). The poem had merely been dropped into a follow-up story on

the Rogers murder but had no connection with it. On September 25, in the New York *Weekly Herald,* the two poems appeared on the front page in adjacent columns. It seems probable that the legend has borrowed Clarke's lines and Halleck's name.

16. H. Allen, *Israfel,* p. 331. Gowans was a lodger in the boardinghouse maintained at this time on Carmine Street by Poe's mother-in-law, Mrs. Clemm. For more on Gowans, see A. H. Quinn's *Poe,* p. 267.

17. Copied except for a change of one word, in *Commercial Advertiser,* October 5, 1838.

18. Copied verbatim in *Commercial Advertiser* the same day.

19. The New York *Journal of Commerce,* August 26, 1841, reported: "We have heard a very different version . . . that she felt so annoyed at such a report having got abroad, during her temporary absence, on a country excursion, that she positively refused ever to return to the store." The *Atlas,* on August 12, 1841, said she quit in a huff, but that Anderson persuaded her to return.

20. New York *Brother Jonathan,* August 14, 1841. The hoax angle was asserted unequivocally about a year later by the *Tragic Almanack* for 1843. It stated that reporters customarily gathered at Anderson's store and "one of them for a joke got out the rumor that the 'Beautiful Cigar Girl' had been seduced—run away with." The publisher of the *Almanack,* C. P. Huestis, had offices at 104 Nassau Street, in the same block as Mary's house. (I am grateful to Thomas M. McDade for supplying a copy of this *Almanack,* a very rare item.)

21. *Herald,* August 17, 1841. The name is also given as Carter; no first name was supplied. On August 18 the *Herald* cleared him of any complicity. Observe that Canter's paper, the *Journal of Commerce,* expressed a belief, almost in personal terms, of Mary's entire innocence of any connection with the 1838 affair (Note 19 above).

22. *Atlas,* August 10, 1841.

23. The *Tribune,* August 19, 1841, claims to record the manner of his death but cites no authority: "Her son . . . was some months ago knocked overboard from a vessel leaving this port and drowned."

24. The New York City *Tax Assessment Records* (Municipal Archives) indicate that the house was put up in 1829 and in 1841 was worth $8,000. It is not clear from the record for 1841 whether Mrs. Rogers owned or rented the place, since her name appears under a column headed "Owner or occupant." The probability is that she rented since this is stated once or twice in passing in contemporary accounts. The same records reveal that the house stood until 1852, when it was replaced by a larger structure of double the value. By 1885 the site, with four or five neighboring lots, had been acquired by William Vanderbilt, who erected an eight-story building worth, in 1890, $325,000.

25. The name is given a wide variety of spellings by the harassed reporters of the day; I adopt this as simplest. According to a Dutch informant of T. O. Mabbott, it was probably *Koekkoek.*

26. Mary's movements that morning, and Payne's for the rest of the day, as

well as Monday, Tuesday and Wednesday, are taken from his deposition to the police, printed in *Weekly Herald,* August 14, 1841. His statements were exhaustively checked at the time.

27. This journeying was not as time-consuming in 1841 as it would be today. Each of these places was within a few minutes' ferry ride of lower Manhattan, and in those days no fewer than a dozen ferries, all of them steam-driven, ringed the tip of the island below Fourteenth Street. Almost forgotten now is the important role played by the New Jersey shore in the recreation of early New Yorkers. In those days regular ads suggested to perspiring city-dwellers "a jaunt to Hoboken" for the "shady and diversified walks . . . invigorating breezes . . . the commanding views presented from the summit of Castle Point . . . the romantic site of the Sybil's Cave . . . the delightful verdure of the Elysian Fields enlivened in the afternoon by an excellent band of music." *(Herald,* August 2, 1842). It was on the Elysian Fields in 1846 that the first real baseball game was played.

28. New York *Sun,* July 28, 1841, p. 3, col. 1.

29. *Herald,* August 4, 1841. The claim of this reporter to being present at the finding of the body, especially a *Herald* reporter, raises some suspicion. It is possible, of course, but it is also possible that he obtained his "eyewitness" account by interviewing persons who actually were there.

30. *Herald,* July 31, 1841.

31. A man named Luther, a friend of Payne's, was present at the discovery of the body, or arrived soon after. It was he who informed Payne. See *Daily Express,* August 3 and 4, 1841.

32. The records of the case in the Hoboken Police Department no longer exist; the regular Hoboken police did not come into being until 1857. The New York police records of the case have also disappeared.

33. She also found her way into Philip Hone's all-embracing diary. An entry for August 6, 1841 reads: "Shocking murder. The body of a young female named Mary Cecilia Rogers was found on Thursday last in the river near Hoboken with horrid marks of violation and violence on her person. . . ." (From the original in the New-York Historical Society). The entry is included in the edition of the diary edited by Allan Nevins (1927), pp. 555, 566-67. Nevins, too, perpetuates the idea that Poe solved the murder: in a note he says "Poe anticipated the solution of the mystery."

34. New York *Advocate of Moral Reform,* September 1, 1841. The paper was published by a "Society of Ladies" at 145 Nassau Street, only a few doors from Mary's house. Its outspoken criticism of Mary's morals may derive from personal knowledge on the part of the "Ladies" but more likely it stems from a general disapproval of girls who ventured too far into the public world, as Mary did when she took the job at Anderson's store.

35. *Herald,* August 13, 1841.

36. The location of the reburial has been something of a minor mystery since the event was sparsely reported in the papers. The official record is in *Register of Deaths, Vol. 12, City Inspector's Department* (Municipal Archives)

under date of August 11, 1841. This identifies the cemetery as the "West Presbyterian"; and the only church by that name in New York in 1841, according to old maps and directories, was the one on Varick Street. Clinching the identification is the fact that one "John Mace" is given as sexton in the *Register* entry and appears in that same capacity in an 1837 brochure of the West Presbyterian Church, as well as in the 1845 edition of Doggett's *The Great Metropolis*. It is a coincidence that Poe, in 1838, had lived only a few doors from this cemetery, at 113½ Carmine Street, where Mrs. Clemm had set up a boardinghouse.

CHAPTER TWO—THE UNSOLVED CASE

1. The body was found by Henry Mallen (Mallin) and James Boulard (Boullard), both of New York City but otherwise unidentifiable and unconnected with the case. *Express,* August 13, 1841, and *Herald,* August 13, 1841.

2. *Herald,* August 17, 1841.

3. *Ibid.*

4. *Tribune,* August 6, 1841; *Express,* August 13, 1841.

5. *Express,* August 12, 1841; *Herald,* August 13, 1841; *Weekly Herald,* August 14, 1841. Suspicion of all four of these men, naturally, was at first intense. Alfred Crommeline, especially, was regarded with a narrow policial eye because of what had happened just before Mary's final disappearance. On Friday, July 23, Mrs. Rogers sent Crommeline a note asking him to call at the house on Nassau Street. He did not respond because of his recent break with Mary and because of the presence of Daniel Payne, whom he resented and regarded as dissipated. Then on Saturday, July 24, Mary herself visited Crommeline's office. Finding him out to lunch, she wrote her name on the visitor's slate (a professional custom of the time) and slipped a rose into the keyhole of the door. Crommeline, in his affidavit, testified that he had not returned the visit. His explanation for all this, checked and accepted by the police, was that Mrs. Rogers had wanted advice on money matters. The rose in the keyhole, however, caught the attention of the press and Crommeline found himself belabored for a week or so, until the police announced their satisfaction with his explanation. Poe, in *Marie Roget,* dismisses the incident as coquettishness on Marie's part toward an old suitor.

6. *Evening Express,* August 14, 1841; *Evening Post,* August 14, 1841.

7. *Herald,* August 17, 1841.

8. *Sun,* August 7, 1841.

9. *Herald,* August 11, 1841; see also *Tribune,* August 10, 1841.

10. *Herald,* August 12, 1841.

11. *Herald,* August 17, 1841.

12. *Tribune,* August 20, 1841; *Morning Courier and New York Enquirer,* August 20, 1841.

13. *Herald,* September 2, 1841, printed Seward's proclamation verbatim: "Whereas Mary C. Rogers, a young woman residing in the City of New York, was lately ravished and murdered in the said city, or in the portion of the State of New Jersey contiguous thereto; and whereas the efforts made by the police of the city of New York to discover the perpetrators of these crimes have, as appears from the public prints, proved altogether unsuccessful; and whereas the peace and security of society require that such atrocious crimes should not go unpunished: Now, therefore, I do hereby declare and make known, that a reward of seven hundred and fifty dollars will be paid to whosoever shall give information resulting in the conviction either in this state or the state of New Jersey, of any person guilty of the said crimes. And I do hereby enjoin upon all magistrates and other ministers of justice, that they be diligent in their efforts to bring the offender or offenders to condign punishment."

The action of the New York aldermen in voting down an additional reward is printed in *Proceedings of the Board of Aldermen,* Vol. 21 (1841), p. 214; the item is easily missed since it does not appear in the index of the *Proceedings.* The original minutes (in the Municipal Archives) of the meeting on September 6 contain nothing further. The resolution, introduced by Alderman Calvin Balis, reads in part: "Whereas great excitement has prevailed in this community and elsewhere in consequence of a most fiend-like outrage and subsequent murder of Mary C. Rogers of this city—and whereas this atrocious, brutal and bloody transaction is enveloped in so much mystery that the magistrates, and officers of the police have thus far been unsuccessful in discovering the perpetrator or perpetrators . . . ." The motion was defeated by a vote of 6 to 10.

14. I have not been able to find Seward's offer of a pardon in the papers, but it is specifically mentioned in *Autobiography of W. H. Seward,* ed. by F. W. Seward (1877), p. 566.

15. Based on a careful sifting and analysis of all the sources detailed in the following notes.

16. *Herald,* September 17, 1841.

17. James Gordon Bennett, predictably, published the letter; *Herald,* September 7, 1841.

18. Lydia Maria Child, *Letters from New York* (1846), pp. 27-32. The date of the letter from which the extract is taken is September 9, 1841.

19. *Herald,* September 17, 1841. The fact that a pair of gloves was found with the other articles in the thicket, as this extract mentions, contradicts the *Herald's* earlier account (see page 19) of the finding of the body with gloves still on the hands. The earlier report must have been mistaken or something more would have been made of this.

20. *Herald,* September 24, 1841. The sites of both inn and thicket are now occupied by the Lincoln Tunnel approach complex. The inn stood almost exactly at the present tunnel entrance; the thicket was located on a (now

obliterated) slope below Willow Avenue, two or three hundred yards north of the present Nineteenth Street.

21. *Herald,* September 24, 1841. This passage very likely provided Poe with the idea for a long paragraph of his own, beginning "An individual has committed the murder. He is alone with the ghost of the departed . . . ." His point in this passage is the same as the *Herald*'s, that the clothes were left behind because the killer was too frightened to return for them. He goes on, however, to show that this indicates no gang did the deed, since a gang would not have hesitated to return and remove the clothes. The irrelevance of this is made clear in my last chapter.

22. Most papers carried reports of Paynes' death. There are long, circumstantial accounts in the *Sun* and the *Tribune* for October 11, 1841. The phial of laudanum found near the thicket bore the name of Souillard and Delluc, a drugstore on Ann Street, which had contributed to the citizens' reward offer. The name "Deluc" in *Marie Roget,* used to designate Mrs. Loss, may have been derived from this source.

CHAPTER THREE—MARY ROGERS BECOMES *Marie*

1. While this is not certain, it is more than probable. The *Shrewsbury Chronicle,* July, 1834, contained an account of an incident involving an orangoutan, trained to climb buildings and rob apartments, being surprised and routed from a bedroom by a woman. Reported by W. Waller in *Notes and Queries,* May 17, 1894:

2. Referring in his *Memoir* to Poe's detective tales, Griswold remarks: "I do not mean to say that they are not ingenious; but they have been thought more ingenious than they are, on account of their method and air of method . . . . What ingenuity is displayed in unravelling a web which has been woven for the express purpose of unravelling? The reader is made to confound the ingenuity at the suppositious Dupin with that of the writer of the story." This comes very close to saying that many readers had begun to credit Poe with the remarkable Dupin's ratiocinative abilities, and this situation lends support to the theory that someone may have urged him to display his powers on an actual mystery.

3. Hirst, it might be noted, later laid claim to a part in the composition of "The Raven," and most biographers concede that he may have contributed a few of its thoughts. Hirst was himself a poet, though a very minor one.

4. There is a tempation, here, to attempt to fill in the biographical vacuum: given some incompatible personal situation on the magazine, could Poe's final decision to leave *Graham's* have been precipitated by a desire to devote full time to *The Mystery of Marie Roget,* in order to finish it as quickly as possible?

5. It is tantalizing to imagine that Dickens himself might have had a hand in impelling Poe to the writing of *Marie Roget,* perhaps by some complimentary remark, during their meetings. It is known that he was impressed by Poe's analytical abilities to the point of commenting that "the man must be the devil." Poe's first review of *Barnaby Rudge,* supposedly anticipating the plot of the novel from a reading of only a few pages, has been much discussed, but the last word seems to have been uttered by Gerald Grubb in an article entitled "The Personal and Literary Relations of Dickens and Poe," *Nineteenth Century Fiction,* June 1950. Grubb shows that Poe's claim in the first review to basing his analysis on a reading of only seven pages is untrue, and that he had probably read at least thirteen chapters. Of the five predictions Poe made in the first review, four were incorrect, and the fifth, though correct, was unimpressive. His claim in the second *Rudge* review that he had been right in the first is pertinent to his actions in the present study of *Marie Roget.*

6. In his discussion of the behavior of drowned bodies in water, though he developed nothing new, Poe appears to have gone beyond the newspapers and consulted some contemporary textbooks on forensic medicine. (Noted by Wimsatt: see Note 14, Chapter 5.)

7. Poe identifies the item, dealing with a supposed rowboat set adrift by the "murderer," as coming from the New York *Standard,* but a search of that paper by Wimsatt (see Note 14, Chapter 5) turned up a blank. The *Herald,* September 24, 1841, has a gratuitous comment on "the spot at the edge of the river, below Ludlow's, where the boat lay in which it is believed the dead body of Mary Rogers was carried into the stream." This could have been enough to prompt Poe to fabrication of his *Standard* paragraph, especially since the use of a boat, in the circumstances of the case, seems natural and, in fact, almost necessary.

8. The statement has no validity even within the context of the story, because of a glaring error which passed unnoticed by Poe. At two widely separated places in the story he refers to the time-lapse between Mary's two "disappearances," but in the first mention he specifies "about five months," and in the other "two or three years." Another curious mistake in the story, carried over unknowingly by Poe from the newspaper accounts, occurs in the description of Marie's body. At the hearing in New York, Dr. Cook stated that "a long slip, say a foot wide, was torn up from the bottom of the frock to the waist, but the piece was not torn off; it was wound three times round the waist." Poe repeats this nearly verbatim, unaware that such a strip from the dress could not have encircled even the smallest-waisted girl more than about one and a half times.

9. Answering an inquiry from George Eveleth, Poe explains that "nothing was omitted in 'Marie Roget' but what I omitted myself:—all *that* is mystification." J. W. Ostrom, *The Letters of Edgar Allan Poe,* II, 355.

10. *Ibid.,* I, 199-200. There seems no clear reason why he should not have offered the tale to *Graham's* despite Rufus Griswold's presence in the editorial chair. Other papers from his pen were printed there in the months

after his resignation. It may be that he did offer it and that it was turned down.

11. *Ibid.,* 201-2.

12. *Herald,* August 12, 1841. The entire list of contributors is given. Among them were Horace Greeley, Richard Adams Locke and Park Benjamin.

13. Ostrom, I, 204, 209.

14. *Ibid.,* II, 356. This derogatory characterization of the *Companion* is rather surprising, especially in view of the magazine's list of contributors, which included Mrs. Sigourney, Rufus Dawes, Samuel Woodworth, N. P. Willis, Park Benjamin, George P. Morris, Mrs. Osgood and W. G. Simms. Poe's *The Landscape Garden* had appeared in the October 1842 issue.

15. *Ibid.,* I, 200.

Chapter Four—Incident at Weehawken

1. A. H. Quinn, *Edgar Allan Poe: A Critical Biography,* pp. 369-70.

2. *Herald,* August 30, 1841; letter from a reader who recalled details of the previous murder on which *Norman Leslie* was based. It was also prominently mentioned in the *Herald,* August 3, 1841.

3. The events connected with the death of Mrs. Loss have been reconstructed from the disjointed testimony elicited at the hearing before Justice Lutkins on November 19, 1842, as reported in *Herald,* November 20, 1842.

4. *Morning Courier and New York Enquirer,* November 12, 1842.

5. A version of it, doctored to suit a distorted solution of the case, was used by Will Clemens in "The Tragedy of Mary Rogers," *Era Magazine,* November 1904, p. 459.

6. *Morning Courier and New York Enquirer,* November 21, 1842; also in *Herald,* November 20, 1842.

7. *Tribune,* November 18, 1842.

8. *Morning Courier and New York Enquirer,* November 18, 1842.

9. *Ibid.,* November 19, 1842.

10. *Herald,* November 20, 1842.

11. *Morning Courier and New York Enquirer,* November 20, 1842.

12. Newark *Daily Advertiser,* November 21, 1842. The New Jersey papers, generally, restricted themselves to copying reports of the case from the New York papers. The belief that Mary Rogers died in the Nick Moore House, whether deliberately murdered or under an abortion is not clear, seems to have persisted in the Weehawken neighborhood for a long time. In 1904 Will Clemens (*Era Magazine,* November 1904) spoke to four elderly people there who remembered the excitement over Mary's death and unhesitatingly connected it with Mrs. Loss and her inn. Clemens gives their names and

addresses, which lends some weight to the only valuable element in an otherwise thoroughly unreliable article.

13. *Tribune,* November 21, 1842.

14. This little contretemps between the *Tribune* and the *Herald* is made too much of by the commentators on the case. It is obvious that the *Tribune* did get hold of something, that it was the wording of its story announcing the confession that was at fault, and that the paper could not, in conscience, make public the names of its highly placed sources. A guess at the identity of one of the "two magistrates" mentioned by the *Tribune* would be Henry W. Merritt, a brother of the Magistrate Gilbert Merritt who was handling the case in New Jersey. Henry Merritt was a magistrate of the Lower Police Court of New York City.

Chapter Five—Mystification

1. From the reminiscences of Poe's friend, F. W. Thomas, quoted in J. H. Whitty's *Memoir,* pp. xlii-xliv (in *The Complete Poems of Edgar Allan Poe,* 1911). The Wistar Lane house still stands, but has long since been engulfed by the growing city. It is tucked into Brandywine Alley, just off Spring Garden Street, at the rear of 530 North Seventh Street. Regarding Poe's poverty, the Philadelphia *Press* (June 19, 1892) records a belief that Mrs. Clemm, sometime in the summer of 1842, applied for aid to a Philadelphia charitable society.

2. In a letter to F. W. Thomas, September 12, 1842, Poe states that "Graham has made me a good offer to return," and indicates that he is toying with the idea. He did not go back to Graham, however, and a letter of September 27, to T. H. Chivers, shows that he was still actively promoting his hoped-for magazine. By October 5, in another letter, he is able to write: "It is my firm determination to commence the 'Penn Magazine' on the first of January next. The difficulties which impeded me last year have vanished, and there will be now nothing to prevent success." The financial operation of the new magazine was tied in with Poe's expected appointment to the Philadelphia Customs House, which would give him a salary to live on, with enough leisure to do his editing. But by November 19, the appointment appeared in jeopardy, and on that date Poe concluded a letter to F. W. Thomas with: "I would write more, my dear Thomas, but my heart is too heavy. You have felt the misery of hope deferred and will feel for me." This was only a day or two before the news of Mrs. Loss's death reached him. (For all four letters, see *Ostrom,* I, 210-19.)

3. The January issue of *The Ladies' Companion* would be printed in the first days of December, and would go on sale about December 15.

4. It is also possible that Snowden himself had decided to cancel the final

instalment and had so informed Poe. In such a case a trip to New York would have been even more imperative, though the necessity would then have been to persuade Snowden that adequate changes were possible. No reason is given in the January issue for the nonappearance of Part Three of *Marie Roget;* neither does any explanation accompany it when it finally does appear in the February issue. A close check of the two issues leads to some interesting if perhaps idle speculation. When *Marie Roget* was pulled from the January issue it left a hole some 10½ columns long (deducting the last two paragraphs which Poe had added—see page 66). As published, the January issue contains ten articles and stories, as well as some poetry. One and only one of the prose pieces is exactly 10½ columns long. It is "The First Love of Henry IV" by, of all people, Mrs. Ellett, who had not at that time met Poe or become his enemy.

5. "Poe's Mary," *Harper's New Monthly Magazine,* March 1889, pp. 634-40. The true identity of this "Mary" has never been stated with certainty. Hervey Allen (p. 427) assumed it was the Mary Devereaux mentioned in J. H. Whitty's *Memoir* (p. xxiv), but Quinn (p. 196) disagrees while claiming to know the real name, though lacking authority to publish it. T. O. Mabbott states that she definitely was Mary (Starr) Devereaux, having been assured of this personally by "Mary's" granddaughter.

6. *Saturday Review of Books and Art,* March 4, 1899, p. 144. Much the same narrative had appeared earlier in the Brooklyn *Daily Eagle,* November 18, 1875 (where the supposed pseudonym was "Thaddeus K. Perley"). Some writers tend to place the Poe-Harrison friendship in 1844 and after, but Harrison clearly mentions an earlier *first* visit.

7. On December 25 he dated a letter to James Russell Lowell from Philadelphia; Ostrom, I, 218.

8. *Ladies' Companion,* XVIII (February 1843), 162-63. The third instalment opens with a lengthy treatment of the thicket at Weehawken, commencing at the paragraph: "Before proceeding further, let us consider the supposed scene of the assassination . . ."

9. W. K. Wimsatt (see Note 14) also noticed the inconsistency here. He remarks: "The arguments against the thicket apply in either case. But Poe has his cake and eats it too—in graceful defiance of the law of contradiction." Wimsatt, however, did not suspect the real cause of the confusion.

10. The letter is quoted in G. E. Woodberry, *Edgar Allan Poe,* II, 83.

11. These events are variously reported in Poe biography. For an announcement of a lecture on American poetry by Poe, see *Evening Mirror,* February 27, 1845, p. 2, which refers to the "Damascene slicing of the critical blade of Mr. Poe." For an account of his connection with the Rutgers Female Institute, see *Evening Mirror,* July 19, 1845.

12. For *Phantasy Pieces,* see Quinn's *Poe,* pp. 336-40. Quinn gives in facsimile Poe's own handwritten table of contents for *Phantasy Pieces;* it shows *The Mystery of Marie Roget* crossed out, signifying, perhaps, an understandable desire to forget the whole thing.

13. A prolific writer and a contributor to Snowden's *Companion,* Ingraham was known to Poe. His novel has no bearing on the real case; it is a sentimental story in which Mary turns up alive at the end.

14. William K. Wimsatt, Jr., "Poe and the Mystery of Mary Rogers," *PMLA,* LVI (March 1941), 230-48. Although he doesn't say so, Wimsatt may have been alerted to Poe's changes by the noncommittal, routine listing of them in the Harrison edition of Poe's works in 1902 (Vol. 4, pp. 313-16). Harrison was not especially interested in *Marie Roget* and merely observes that "some inaccuracies were corrected, the language was harmonized, and objectionable passages eliminated." Although Poe's sleight of hand must have been abundantly clear to Wimsatt, he refers to the changes merely as a "revised conclusion." The extent to which scholarship can blind itself to the clear implication of fact is further demonstrated by A. H. Quinn's remark on Wimsatt's article. Wimsatt, says Quinn, "collects the newspaper accounts and reviews the situation but comes to no conclusion." It should also be noted that Wimsatt seems not to have realized that Poe would certainly have been aware of the break in the case that followed Mrs. Loss's death in November 1842. For some reason, Wimsatt felt that Poe did not hear of the Loss affair until "after he came to New York in 1844, when he mingled with newspapermen."

15. In addition to the changes detailed here, Poe, following his usual practice, made many other small revisions in wording, punctuation, etc.; these, of course, we are not concerned with. For the sake of clarity in the extracts, I have omitted his occasional use of italics. This does not affect the sense in any way. Page numbers in italics at the end of each of the following notes refer the reader to the location of the material in the reprint of Poe's story at the back of this book.

16. *Ladies' Companion,* XVIII (February 1843), p. 164, col. 1. *(p. 134)*

17. *Ibid.,* p. 165, col. 2. *(p. 139)*

18. *Ibid.,* p. 167, col. 1. *(p. 142)*

19. *Ibid.,* (December 1842), p. 98, col. 2. *(p. 127)*

20. *Ibid.*

21. *Ibid. (p. 128)*

22. *Ibid.,* (February 1843), p. 162, col. 1. *(p. 129)*

23. *Ibid.,* p. 163, col. 2 *(p. 134).* This idea of an "accident at Madame Deluc's" is introduced into the text without any preparation or justification in the material that precedes it. The inconsistency usually eludes the casual reader, however, because of the detailed intricacy of the narrative.

24. *Ibid.,* p. 164, col. 1. *(p. 134)*

25. *Ibid.,* p. 165, col. 1. *(p. 137)*

26. *Ibid.*

27. *Ibid.,* This insertion has not been noted previously.

28. *Ibid.,* p. 165, col. 2. *(p. 139)*

29. *Ibid.*

30. *Ibid.,* p. 166, col. 1. *(p. 140)*

31. Poe's notes give no dates for the extracts, and the story itself alters both actual dates and authentic time-spans. Despite this, Wimsatt was able to find approximate originals for some of the stories he adapted. A difficulty in tracing the exact sources of the paragraphs is the great amount of indiscriminate reprinting in Poe's day, making almost impossible to be sure precisely where he may have found an item.

32. It is interesting to speculate that Poe's story might, after all, have played a part, though in a totally unintended and unanticipated way, in the solution of the mystery. The first instalment of *Marie Roget* appeared in the *Companion*'s November issue, which reached the public in mid-October, and two weeks later there occurred the fatal shooting of Mrs. Loss by one of her sons. There was nothing in that first instalment to cause the Loss family any specific uneasiness, but it is conceivable that the air of confidence in the tale, and its detailed analytical progression, may have alarmed them about what was to come, the alarm ending somehow in the shooting.

33. The pardon offered by Governor Seward (see Note 14, Chapter 2) could have played a part here. Crommeline's rather shadowy part in the story makes it seem that he may have been more deeply involved than has appeared, and it may have been he who later supplied further information. Mary's visit to his office the day before she was to undergo an abortion, and her leaving a rose in the keyhole (see Note 5, Chapter 2) gives some legitimate reason for pause. He knew the girl was missing on Monday, July 26, and Tuesday, July 27, but did not begin searching until Wednesday, July 28, when her disappearance became public knowledge through the ad placed in the *Sun* by Payne. And then he immediately began his quest along the Jersey shore. There is the possibility, at least, that it was Crommeline who arranged the abortion for Mary and that on the Monday and Tuesday of her "disappearance" he still believed or hoped that she would return safely. He may have been on his way to the Nick Moore house, expecting to find Mary recuperating, when he encountered the crowd on the shore clustering round her body.

34. To Eveleth, in 1848, Poe wrote: "The 'naval officer' who committed the murder (or rather the accidental death arising from an attempt at abortion) *confessed* it; and the whole matter is now well understood—but for the sake of relatives, this is a topic on which I must not speak further." Ostrom, II, 355-56.

35. I have tried hard to find some mitigating reason for Poe's putting forth such an obviously false claim. He was not at heart a conscious and deliberate liar, but was of the type that finds it easy to make large and sweeping pronouncements from the slimmest justification and merest coincidences. It appears to me that in his long discussion of the Weehawken thicket as the scene of the crime, where he contends that the evidence pointed to a single assassin and not a gang, he may have felt that he had anticipated the truth about the clothes in the thicket—that they had been placed there later. But even his discussion of these things was not entirely original with him; doubts about the thicket as the scene of the crime were widely expressed (cf. *Brother*

Jonathan, September 25, 1842) and what Poe did was to bring them together and express them lucidly. Slim justification indeed.

36. E. M. Bacon, *The Hudson River,* p. 80.

37. D. E. S. Maxwell, *American Fiction: The Intellectual Background,* pp. 95-96. The observation occurs in a lengthy footnote.

EPILOGUE—SOME LOOSE ENDS

1. Charles Wallace, *A Confession of the Awful Bloody Transactions in the Life of the Fiend-like Murderer of Miss Mary Rogers, the Beautiful Cigar Girl of Broadway, etc.,* told to Rev. Henry Tracy (New Orleans, E. E. Barclay & Co., 1851). The pamphlet is a good example of the phony confessions that followed almost every crime of note in the early nineteenth century; Mary Rogers' murder is only one of a number of dark deeds confessed. Copies are at the Library of Congress and New York Public Library.

2. Davis was an acquaintance of Poe's. His novel, however, contains nothing pertinent to the real case, except that its portrayal of an abortion death supports the probable truth.

3. J. H. Ingram, *Poe,* p. 235.

4. "The Mystery of Mary Rogers," *Collier's Magazine,* March 8, 1930.

5. W. K. Wimsatt, *PMLA,* March 1941, p. 247.

6. I. Wallace, *Fabulous Originals,* p. 206. Wallace implies, erroneously, that Wimsatt considered Philip Spencer a legitimate suspect, but this is the least of a large number of distortions and inaccuracies in Wallace's treatment.

7. F. Van de Water, *The Captain Called It Mutiny,* pp. 27-32. Spencer was expelled from Geneva College in April 1841 for "neglect of college exercises," after which he enrolled briefly in Union College. His father, U.S. Secretary of War John C. Spencer, procured him an appointment as midshipman, and he joined the receiving ship *North Carolina* in the Brooklyn Navy Yard, on November 20, 1841. Here, he made his closest approach to the Rogers case, for William Kiekuck had been serving on board the *North Carolina* when he was twice questioned by police in August 1841.

8. H. Hayford, *The Somers Mutiny Affair,* pp. 2-7.

9. In the Ingram papers at the University of Virginia there is a letter from Helen Whitman to George Eveleth, dated March 2, 1867, and a fragment of a copy of this letter, made for Ingram and dated October 1, 1878. In her letter, Mrs. Whitman says Poe told her that "the name of the young naval officer was Spencer." *John Henry Ingram's Poe Collection at the University of Virginia,* by John C. Miller (Univ. of Virginia Press, 1960), p. 30.

Though the item is interesting, it poses insurmountable problems: How dependable was Mrs. Whitman's memory after so many years? Did Poe specify the name as that of a naval officer, or was that just Mrs. Whitman's way of putting it? If Poe did make such a remark to Mrs. Whitman, it was probably in 1848-49, about the same time he was writing to Eveleth (see Note 34, Chapter 5) and equating the term "naval officer" with "abortionist," so even if he specified a naval officer to Mrs. Whitman it probably did not have the meaning she took. If Mrs. Whitman is dependable regarding the name, and if Poe did not pick it out of thin air, then he meant the abortionist was named Spencer, but that is as far as the trail leads. There may, in fact, have been no other abortionist than Mrs. Loss herself.

10. The main facts about Anderson's career are from two articles by lawyer Samuel Copp Worthen: *Proceedings of the New Jersey Historical Society,* April 1942, and *American Literature,* November 1948. Worthen was a member of the law firm that possessed the original records of the suit brought in 1891 by Anderson's daughter, Laura Appleton. The action was settled out of court the following year, so the record was never printed. Worthen has no mention of earlier suits brought by other Anderson heirs, the records of which have been lost. In addition to Worthen's articles, information has also been gathered from three brief newspaper accounts of the continuing litigation: New York *Times,* October 16, 1885; New York *Tribune,* May 27, 1887, and January 11, 1892.

11. New York City *Tax Assessment Records* (see Note 24, Chapter 1).

12. Mention of a possible earlier abortion prompted Worthen to connect it with Mary Rogers' 1838 "disappearance," as did William Wimsatt in *American Literature,* January 1950, pp. 482-84. But this is simply guessing, and the 1838 affair seems best explained as I have presented it, that is, as a crude practical joke. If Mary did undergo a first abortion sometime in 1839 or 1840, then her short life and mournful death appears as a sad corroboration of the fears expressed by many people at the time over "very beautiful young girls being placed in cigar and confectionary stores."

13. The earliest mention of this occurred during the Anderson will litigation. A witness, a journalist friend of Anderson's named Andrew Wheeler, under examination denied any knowledge of such a possibility. It was all part of the attempt to prove Anderson's incompetence (see *Tribune,* May 27, 1887). No idea, it seems is too extraordinary for Poe and the Mary Rogers case, but this one is far-fetched indeed. Poe did not offer his story for publication until June 1842, at which time the Rogers case had been dormant for eight months. Moreover, in attempting to link Mary's death with the incident of her first disappearance in 1838, Poe unavoidably brought into the forefront her connection with Anderson's store; this was hardly drawing attention away from the tobacconist. And Poe's reference in the tale to Anderson's clientele was decidedly less than favorable: it was to be found, he wrote, "chiefly among the desperate adventurers infesting that neighborhood." If there is any bit of truth to the notion at all, it may have to do with Anderson's relationship with the city's publishers and journalists, many of whom frequented his store. Could he have been in some way instrumental in getting the story published in the *Companion?*

The Mystery of Marie Roget

BY Edgar Allan Poe

(The final version, as published in *Tales*, 1845)

The Mystery of Marie Roget*

A SEQUEL TO "THE MURDERS IN THE RUE MORGUE."

Es giebt eine Reihe idealischer Begebenheiten, die der Wirklichkeit parallel lauft. Selten fallen sie zusammen. Menschen und zufalle modificiren gewohnlich die idealische Begebenheit, so dass sie unvollkommen erscheint, und ihre Folgen gleichfalls unvollkommen sind. So bei der Reformation; statt des Protestantismus kam das Lutherthum hervor.

There are ideal series of events which run parallel with the real ones. They rarely coincide. Men and circumstances generally modify the ideal train of events, so that it seems imperfect, and its consequences are equally imperfect. Thus with the Reformation; instead of Protestantism came Lutheranism.— Novalis.† Moral Ansichten.

THERE are few persons, even among the calmest thinkers, who have not occasionally been startled into a vague yet thrilling half-credence in the supernatural, by *coincidences* of so seemingly marvellous a character that, as *mere* coincidences, the intellect has been unable to receive them. Such sentiments—for the half-credences of which I speak have never the

---

*Upon the original publication of "Marie Rogêt," the foot-notes now appended were considered unnecessary; but the lapse of several years since the tragedy upon which the tale is based, renders it expedient to give them, and also to say a few words in explanation of the general design. A young girl, *Mary Cecilia Rogers*, was murdered in the vicinity of New York; and, although her death occasioned an intense and long-enduring excitement, the mystery attending it had remained unsolved at the period when the present paper was written and published (November, 1842). Herein, under pretence of relating the fate of a Parisian *grisette*, the author has followed, in minute detail, the essential, while merely paralleling the inessential facts of the real murder of Mary Rogers. Thus all argument founded upon the fiction is applicable to the truth: and the investigation of the truth was the object.

The "Mystery of Marie Rogêt" was composed at a distance from the scene of the atrocity, and with no other means of investigation than the newspapers afforded. Thus

†The *nom de plume* of Von Hardenburg.

full force of *thought*—such sentiments are seldom thoroughly stifled unless by reference to the doctrine of chance, or, as it is technically termed, the Calculus of Probabilities. Now this Calculus is, in its essence, purely mathematical; and thus we have the anomaly of the most rigidly exact in science applied to the shadow and spirituality of the most intangible in speculation.

The extraordinary details which I am now called upon to make public, will be found to form, as regards sequence of time, the primary branch of a series of scarcely intelligible *coincidences,* whose secondary or concluding branch will be recognized by all readers in the late murder of MARY CECILIA ROGERS, at New York.

When, in an article entitled "The Murders in the Rue Morgue," I endeavored, about a year ago, to depict some very remarkable features in the mental character of my friend, the Chevalier C. Auguste Dupin, it did not occur to me that I should ever resume the subject. This depicting of character constituted my design; and this design was thoroughly fulfilled in the wild train of circumstances brought to instance Dupin's idiosyncrasy. I might have adduced other examples, but I should have proven no more. Late events, however, in their surprising development, have startled me into some farther details, which will carry with them the air of extorted confession. Hearing what I have lately heard, it would be indeed strange should I remain silent in regard to what I both heard and saw so long ago.

Upon the winding up of the tragedy involved in the deaths of Madame L'Espanaye and her daughter, the Chevalier dismissed the affair at once from his attention, and relapsed into his old habits of moody reverie. Prone, at all times, to abstraction, I readily fell in with his humor; and, continuing to occupy our chambers in the Faubourg Saint Germain, we gave the Future to the winds, and slumbered tranquilly in the Present, weaving the dull world around us into dreams.

---

much escaped the writer of which he could have availed himself had he been upon the spot, and visited the localities. It may not be improper to record, nevertheless, that the confessions of *two* persons, (one of them the Madame Deluc of the narrative) made, at different periods, long subsequent to the publication, confirmed, in full, not only the general conclusion, but absolutely *all* the chief hypothetical details by which that conclusion was attained.

But these dreams were not altogether uninterrupted. It may readily be supposed that the part played by my friend, in the drama at the Rue Morgue, had not failed of its impression upon the fancies of the Parisian police. With its emissaries, the name of Dupin had grown into a household word. The simple character of those inductions by which he had disentangled the mystery never having been explained even to the Prefect, or to any other individual than myself, of course it is not surprising that the affair was regarded as little less than miraculous, or that the Chevalier's analytical abilities acquired for him the credit of intuition. His frankness would have led him to disabuse every inquirer of such prejudice; but his indolent humor forbade all farther agitation of a topic whose interest to himself had long ceased. It thus happened that he found himself the cynosure of the policial eyes; and the cases were not few in which attempt was made to engage his services at the Prefecture. One of the most remarkable instances was that of the murder of a young girl named Marie Rogêt.

This event occurred about two years after the atrocity in the Rue Morgue. Marie, whose Christian and family name will at once arrest attention from their resemblance to those of the unfortunate "cigar-girl," was the only daughter of the widow Estelle Rogêt. The father had died during the child's infancy, and from the period of his death, until within eighteen months before the assassination which forms the subject of our narrative, the mother and daughter had dwelt together in the Rue Pavée Saint Andrée;* Madame there keeping a *pension,* assisted by Marie. Affairs went on thus until the latter had attained her twenty-second year, when her great beauty attracted the notice of a perfumer, who occupied one of the shops in the basement of the Palais Royal, and whose custom lay chiefly among the desperate adventurers infesting that neighborhood. Monsieur Le Blanc† was not unaware of the advantages to be derived from the attendance of the fair Marie in his perfumery; and his liberal proposals were accepted eagerly by the girl, although with somewhat more of hesitation by Madame.

The anticipations of the shopkeeper were realized, and his rooms soon became notorious through the charms of the sprightly *grisette.*

*Nassau Street.
†Anderson.

She had been in his employ about a year, when her admirers were thrown into confusion by her sudden disappearance from the shop. Monsieur Le Blanc was unable to account for her absence, and Madame Rogêt was distracted with anxiety and terror. The public papers immediately took up the theme, and the police were upon the point of making serious investigations, when, one fine morning, after the lapse of a week, Marie, in good health, but with a somewhat saddened air, made her re-appearance at her usual counter in the perfumery. All inquiry, except that of a private character, was of course immediately hushed. Monsieur Le Blanc professed total ignorance, as before. Marie, with Madame, replied to all questions, that the last week had been spent at the house of a relation in the country. Thus the affair died away, and was generally forgotten; for the girl, ostensibly to relieve herself from the impertinence of curiosity, soon bade a final adieu to the perfumer, and sought the shelter of her mother's residence in the Rue Pavée Saint Andrée.

It was about five months after this return home, that her friends were alarmed by her sudden disappearance for the second time. Three days elapsed, and nothing was heard of her. On the fourth her corpse was found floating in the Seine,* near the shore which is opposite the Quartier of the Rue Saint Andrée, and at a point not very far distant from the secluded neighborhood of the Barrière du Roule.†

The atrocity of this murder, (for it was at once evident that murder had been committed,) the youth and beauty of the victim, and, above all, her previous notoriety, conspired to produce intense excitement in the minds of the sensitive Parisians. I can call to mind no similar occurrence producing so general and so intense an effect. For several weeks, in the discussion of this one absorbing theme, even the momentous political topics of the day were forgotten. The Prefect made unusual exertions; and the powers of the whole Parisian police were, of course, tasked to the utmost extent.

Upon the first discovery of the corpse, it was not supposed that the murderer would be able to elude, for more than a very brief period, the inquisition which was immediately set on foot. It was

*The Hudson.
†Weehawken.

not until the expiration of a week that it was deemed necessary to offer a reward; and even then this reward was limited to a thousand francs. In the mean time the investigation proceeded with vigor, if not always with judgment, and numerous individuals were examined to no purpose; while, owing to the continual absence of all clue to the mystery, the popular excitement greatly increased. At the end of the tenth day it was thought advisable to double the sum originally proposed; and, at length, the second week having elapsed without leading to any discoveries, and the prejudice which always exists in Paris against the Police having given vent to itself in several serious *émeutes,* the Prefect took it upon himself to offer the sum of twenty thousand francs "for the conviction of the assassin," or, if more than one should prove to have been implicated, "for the conviction of any one of the assassins." In the proclamation setting forth this reward, a full pardon was promised to any accomplice who should come forward in evidence against his fellow; and to the whole was appended, wherever it appeared, the private placard of a committee of citizens, offering ten thousand francs, in addition to the amount proposed by the Prefecture. The entire reward thus stood at no less than thirty thousand francs, which will be regarded as an extraordinary sum when we consider the humble condition of the girl, and the great frequency, in large cities, of such atrocities as the one described.

No one doubted now that the mystery of this murder would be immediately brought to light. But although, in one or two instances, arrests were made which promised elucidation, yet nothing was elicited which could implicate the parties suspected; and they were discharged forthwith. Strange as it may appear, the third week from the discovery of the body had passed, and passed without any light being thrown upon the subject, before even a rumor of the events which had so agitated the public mind, reached the ears of Dupin and myself. Engaged in researches which had absorbed our whole attention, it had been nearly a month since either of us had gone abroad, or received a visiter, or more than glanced at the leading political articles in one of the daily papers. The first intelligence of the murder was brought us by G——, in person. He called upon us early in the afternoon of the thirteenth of July, 18—, and remained with us until late in the night. He had been piqued by the failure of all his endeavors to ferret out the assassins. His reputation—so he said with a peculiarly Parisian air—was at stake. Even his honor was concerned. The eyes of the public were upon him; and there was really no sacrifice which he would not be willing to make for the development of the mystery. He concluded a somewhat droll speech with a compliment upon what he was pleased to term the *tact* of Dupin, and made him a direct, and certainly a liberal proposition, the precise nature of which I do not feel myself at liberty to disclose, but which has no bearing upon the proper subject of my narrative.

The compliment my friend rebutted as best he could, but the proposition he accepted at once, although its advantages were altogether provisional. This point being settled, the Prefect broke forth at once into explanations of his own views, interspersing them with long comments upon the evidence; of which latter we were not yet in possession. He discoursed much, and beyond doubt, learnedly; while I hazarded an occasional suggestion as the night wore drowsily away. Dupin, sitting steadily in his accustomed arm-chair, was the embodiment of respectful attention. He wore spectacles, during the whole interview; and an occasional glance beneath their green glasses, sufficed to convince me that he slept not the less soundly, because silently, throughout the seven or eight leaden-footed hours which immediately preceded the departure of the Prefect.

In the morning, I procured, at the Prefecture, a full report of all the evidence elicited, and, at the various newspaper offices, a copy of every paper in which, from first to last, had been published any decisive information in regard to this sad affair. Freed from all that was positively disproved, this mass of information stood thus:

Marie Rogêt left the residence of her mother, in the Rue Pavée St. Andrée, about nine o'clock in the morning of Sunday, June the twenty-second, 18—. In going out, she gave notice to a Monsieur Jacques St. Eustache,* and to him only, of her intention to spend the day with an aunt who resided in the Rue des Drômes. The Rue des Drômes is a short and narrow but populous thoroughfare, not far from the banks of the river, and at a distance of some two miles, in the most direct course possible, from the *pension* of Madame Rogêt. St. Eustache was the accepted suitor of Marie, and lodged, as

*Payne.

well as took his meals, at the *pension*. He was to have gone for his
betrothed at dusk, and to have escorted her home. In the afternoon,
however, it came on to rain heavily; and, supposing that she would
remain all night at her aunt's, (as she had done under similar
circumstances before,) he did not think it necessary to keep his
promise. As night drew on, Madame Rogêt (who was an infirm old
lady, seventy years of age,) was heard to express a fear "that she
should never see Marie again;" but this observation attracted little
attention at the time.

On Monday, it was ascertained that the girl had not been to the
Rue des Drômes; and when the day elapsed without tidings of her, a
tardy search was instituted at several points in the city, and its
environs. It was not, however, until the fourth day from the period
of her disappearance that any thing satisfactory was ascertained
respecting her. On this day, (Wednesday, the twenty-fifth of June,)
a Monsieur Beauvais,* who, with a friend, had been making
inquiries for Marie near the Barrière du Roule, on the shore of the
Seine which is opposite the Rue Pavée St. Andrée, was informed
that a corpse had just been towed ashore by some fishermen, who
had found it floating in the river. Upon seeing the body, Beauvais,
after some hesitation, identified it as that of the perfumery-girl. His
friend recognized it more promptly.

The face was suffused with dark blood, some of which issued from
the mouth. No foam was seen, as in the case of the merely drowned.
There was no discoloration in the cellular tissue. About the throat
were bruises and impressions of fingers. The arms were bent over on
the chest and were rigid. The right hand was clenched; the left
partially open. On the left wrist were two circular excoriations,
apparently the effect of ropes, or of a rope in more than one
volution. A part of the right wrist, also, was much chafed, as well as
the back throughout its extent, but more especially at the shoulder-
blades. In bringing the body to the shore the fishermen had attached
to it a rope, but none of the excoriations had been effected by this.
The flesh of the neck was much swollen. There were no cuts
apparent, or bruises which appeared the effect of blows. A piece of
lace was found tied so tightly around the neck as to be hidden from
sight; it was completely buried in the flesh, and was fastened by a

*Crommelin.

knot which lay just under the left ear. This alone would have sufficed to produce death. The medical testimony spoke confidently of the virtuous character of the deceased. She had been subjected, it said, to brutal violence. The corpse was in such condition when found, that there could have been no difficulty in its recognition by friends.

The dress was much torn and otherwise disordered. In the outer garment, a slip, about a foot wide, had been torn upward from the bottom hem to the waist, but not torn off. It was wound three times around the waist, and secured by a sort of hitch in the back. The dress immediately beneath the frock was of fine muslin; and from this a slip eighteen inches wide had been torn entirely out—torn very evenly and with great care. It was found around her neck, fitting loosely, and secured with a hard knot. Over this muslin slip and the slip of lace, the strings of a bonnet were attached; the bonnet being appended. The knot by which the strings of the bonnet were fastened, was not a lady's, but a slip or sailor's knot.

After the recognition of the corpse, it was not, as usual, taken to the Morgue, (this formality being superfluous,) but hastily interred not far from the spot at which it was brought ashore. Through the exertions of Beauvais, the matter was industriously hushed up, as far as possible; and several days had elapsed before any public emotion resulted. A weekly paper,* however at length took up the theme; the corpse was disinterred, and a re-examination instituted; but nothing was elicited beyond what has been already noted. The clothes, however, were now submitted to the mother and friends of the deceased, and fully identified as those worn by the girl upon leaving home.

Meantime, the excitement increased hourly. Several individuals were arrested and discharged. St. Eustache fell especially under suspicion; and he failed, at first, to give an intelligible account of his whereabouts during the Sunday on which Marie left home. Subsequently, however, he submitted to Monsieur G——, affidavits, accounting satisfactorily for every hour of the day in question. As time passed and no discovery ensued, a thousand contradictory rumors were circulated, and journalists busied themselves in *suggestions.* Among these, the one which attracted the most notice,

*The "N. Y. Mercury."

was the idea that Marie Rogêt still lived—that the corpse found in the Seine was that of some other unfortunate. It will be proper that I submit to the reader some passages which embody the suggestion alluded to. These passages are *literal* translations from L'Etoile,* a paper conducted, in general, with much ability.

"Mademoiselle Rogêt left her mother's house on Sunday morning, June the twenty-second, 18—, with the ostensible purpose of going to see her aunt, or some other connexion, in the Rue des Drômes. From that hour, nobody is proved to have seen her. There is no trace or tidings of her at all. * * * * There has no person, whatever, come forward, so far, who saw her at all, on that day, after she left her mother's door. * * * * Now, though we have no evidence that Marie Rogêt was in the land of the living after nine o'clock on Sunday, June the twenty-second, we have proof that, up to that hour, she was alive. On Wednesday noon, at twelve, a female body was discovered afloat on the shore of the Barrière du Roule. This was, even if we presume that Marie Rogêt was thrown into the river within three hours after she left her mother's house, only three days from the time she left her home—three days to an hour. But it is folly to suppose that the murder, if murder was committed on her body, could have been consummated soon enough to have enabled her murderers to throw the body into the river before midnight. Those who are guilty of such horrid crimes, choose darkness rather than light. * * * * Thus we see that if the body found in the river *was* that of Marie Rogêt, it could only have been in the water two and a half days, or three at the outside. All experience has shown that drowned bodies, or bodies thrown into the water immediately after death by violence, require from six to ten days for sufficient decomposition to take place to bring them to the top of the water. Even where a cannon is fired over a corpse, and it rises before at least five or six days' immersion, it sinks again, if let alone. Now, we ask, what was there in this case to cause a departure from the ordinary course of nature? * * * * If the body had been kept in its mangled state on shore until Tuesday night, some trace would be found on shore of the murderers. It is a doubtful point, also, whether the body would be so soon afloat, even were it thrown in after having been dead two days. And, furthermore, it is exceedingly improbable that any villains who had committed such a murder as is here supposed, would have thrown the body in without weight to sink it, when such a precaution could have so easily been taken."

The editor here proceeds to argue that the body must have been in the water "not three days merely, but, at least, five times three days," because it was so far decomposed that Beauvais had great

*The "N. Y. Brother Jonathan," edited by H. Hastings Weld, Esq.

difficulty in recognizing it. This latter point, however, was fully
disproved. I continue the translation:

> "What, then, are the facts on which M. Beauvais says that he has no doubt
> the body was that of Marie Rogêt? He ripped up the gown sleeve, and says
> he found marks which satisfied him of the identity. The public generally
> supposed those marks to have consisted of some description of scars. He
> rubbed the arm and found *hair* upon it—something as indefinite, we think,
> as can readily be imagined—as little conclusive as finding an arm in the
> sleeve. M. Beauvais did not return that night, but sent word to Madame
> Rogêt, at seven o'clock, on Wednesday evening, that an investigation was
> still in progress respecting her daughter. If we allow that Madame Rogêt,
> from her age and grief, could not go over, (which is allowing a great deal,)
> there certainly must have been some one who would have thought it worth
> while to go over and attend the investigation, if they thought the body was
> that of Marie. Nobody went over. There was nothing said or heard about
> the matter in the Rue Pavée St. Andrée, that reached even the occupants
> of the same building. M. St. Eustache, the lover and intended husband of
> Marie, who boarded in her mother's house, deposes that he did not hear of
> the discovery of the body of his intended until the next morning, when M.
> Beauvais came into his chamber and told him of it. For an item of news
> like this, it strikes us it was very coolly received."

In this way the journal endeavored to create the impression of an
apathy on the part of the relatives of Marie, inconsistent with the
supposition that these relatives believed the corpse to be hers. Its
insinuations amount to this:—that Marie, with the connivance of
her friends, had absented herself from the city for reasons involving
a charge against her chastity; and that these friends, upon the
discovery of a corpse in the Seine, somewhat resembling that of the
girl, had availed themselves of the opportunity to impress the public
with the belief of her death. But L'Etoile was again over-hasty. It
was distinctly proved that no apathy, such as was imagined, existed;
that the old lady was exceedingly feeble, and so agitated as to be
unable to attend to any duty; that St. Eustache, so far from
receiving the news coolly, was distracted with grief, and bore himself
so frantically, that M. Beauvais prevailed upon a friend and relative
to take charge of him, and prevent his attending the examination at
the disinterment. Moreover, although it was stated by L'Etoile, that
the corpse was re-interred at the public expense—that an
advantageous offer of private sepulture was absolutely declined by
the family—and that no member of the family attended the

ceremonial:—although, I say, all this was asserted by L'Etoile in furtherance of the impression it designed to convey—yet *all* this was satisfactorily disproved. In a subsequent number of the paper, an attempt was made to throw suspicion upon Beauvais himself. The editor says:

> "Now, then, a change comes over the matter. We are told that, on one occasion, while a Madame B—— was at Madame Rogêt's house, M. Beauvais, who was going out, told her that a *gendarme* was expected there, and that she, Madame B., must not say anything to the *gendarme* until he returned, but let the matter be for him. * * * * In the present posture of affairs, M. Beauvais appears to have the whole matter locked up in his head. A single step cannot be taken without M. Beauvais; for, go which way you will, you run against him. * * * * * For some reason, he determined that nobody shall have any thing to do with the proceedings but himself, and he has elbowed the male relatives out of the way, according to their representations, in a very singular manner. He seems to have been very much averse to permitting the relatives to see the body."

By the following fact, some color was given to the suspicion thus thrown upon Beauvais. A visiter at his office, a few days prior to the girl's disappearance, and during the absence of its occupant, had observed *a rose* in the key-hole of the door, and the name *"Marie"* inscribed upon a slate which hung near at hand.

The general impression, so far as we were enabled to glean it from the newspapers, seemed to be, that Marie had been the victim of *a gang* of desperadoes—that by these she had been borne across the river, maltreated and murdered. Le Commerciel,* however, a print of extensive influence, was earnest in combating this popular idea. I quote a passage or two from its columns:

> "We are persuaded that pursuit has hitherto been on a false scent, so far as it has been directed to the Barrière du Roule. It is impossible that a person so well known to thousands as this young woman was, should have passed three blocks without some one having seen her; and any one who saw her would have remembered it, for she interested all who knew her. It was when the streets were full of people, when she went out. * * * It is impossible that she could have gone to the Barrière du Roule, or to the Rue des Drômes, without being recognized by a dozen persons; yet no one has come forward who saw her outside of her mother's door, and there is no evidence, except the testimony concerning her *expressed intentions,* that she did go out at all. Her gown was torn, bound round her, and tied; and

*N. Y. "Journal of Commerce."

by that the body was carried as a bundle. If the murder had been committed at the Barrière du Roule, there would have been no necessity for any such arrangement. The fact that the body was found floating near the Barrière, is no proof as to where it was thrown into the water. *   *   *   *   *   A piece of one of the unfortunate girl's petticoats, two feet long and one foot wide, was torn out and tied under her chin around the back of her head, probably to prevent screams. This was done by fellows who had no pocket-handkerchief."

A day or two before the Prefect called upon us, however, some important information reached the police, which seemed to overthrow, at least, the chief portion of Le Commerciel's argument. Two small boys, sons of a Madame Deluc, while roaming among the woods near the Barrière du Roule, chanced to penetrate a close thicket, within which were three or four large stones, forming a kind of seat, with a back and footstool. On the upper stone lay a white petticoat; on the second a silk scarf. A parasol, gloves, and a pocket-handkerchief were also here found. The handkerchief bore the name "Marie Rogêt." Fragments of dress were discovered on the brambles around. The earth was trampled, the bushes were broken, and there was every evidence of a struggle. Between the thicket and the river, the fences were found taken down, and the ground bore evidence of some heavy burthen having been dragged along it.

A weekly paper, Le Soleil,* had the following comments upon this discovery—comments which merely echoed the sentiment of the whole Parisian press:

"The things had all evidently been there at least three or four weeks; they were all mildewed down hard with the action of the rain, and stuck together from mildew. The grass had grown around and over some of them. The silk on the parasol was strong, but the threads of it were run together within. The upper part, where it had been doubled and folded, was all mildewed and rotten, and tore on its being opened. * * * * The pieces of her frock torn out by the bushes were about three inches wide and six inches long. One part was the hem of the frock, and it had been mended; the other piece was part of the skirt, not the hem. They looked like strips torn off, and were on the thorn bush, about a foot from the ground. *   *   *   * There can be no doubt, therefore, that the spot of this appalling outrage has been discovered."

Consequent upon this discovery, new evidence appeared. Madame Deluc testified that she keeps a roadside inn not far from the bank

*Phil. "Sat. Evening Post," edited by C. I. Peterson, Esq.

of the river, opposite the Barrière du Roule. The neighborhood is secluded—particularly so. It is the usual Sunday resort of blackguards from the city, who cross the river in boats. About three o'clock, in the afternoon of the Sunday in question, a young girl arrived at the inn, accompanied by a young man of dark complexion. The two remained here for some time. On their departure, they took the road to some thick woods in the vicinity. Madame Deluc's attention was called to the dress worn by the girl, on account of its resemblance to one worn by a deceased relative. A scarf was particularly noticed. Soon after the departure of the couple, a gang of miscreants made their appearance, behaved boisterously, ate and drank without making payment, followed in the route of the young man and girl, returned to the inn about dusk, and re-crossed the river as if in great haste.

It was soon after dark, upon this same evening, that Madame Deluc, as well as her eldest son, heard the screams of a female in the vicinity of the inn. The screams were violent but brief. Madame D. recognized not only the scarf which was found in the thicket, but the dress which was discovered upon the corpse. An omnibus-driver, Valence,* now also testified that he saw Marie Rogêt cross a ferry on the Seine, on the Sunday in question, in company with a young man of dark complexion. He, Valence, knew Marie, and could not be mistaken in her identity. The articles found in the thicket were fully identified by the relatives of Marie.

The items of evidence and information thus collected by myself, from the newspapers, at the suggestion of Dupin, embraced only one more point—but this was a point of seemingly vast consequence. It appears that, immediately after the discovery of the clothes as above described, the lifeless, or nearly lifeless body of St. Eustache, Marie's betrothed, was found in the vicinity of what all now supposed the scene of the outrage. A phial labelled "laudanum," and emptied, was found near him. His breath gave evidence of the poison. He died without speaking. Upon his person was found a letter, briefly stating his love for Marie, with his design of self-destruction.

"I need scarcely tell you," said Dupin, as he finished the perusal of my notes, "that this is a far more intricate case than that of the Rue Morgue; from which it differs in one important respect. This is an

*Adam.

ordinary, although an atrocious instance of crime. There is nothing peculiarly *outré* about it. You will observe that, for this reason, the mystery has been considered easy, when, for this reason, it should have been considered difficult, of solution. Thus, at first, it was thought unnecessary to offer a reward. The myrmidons of G—— were able at once to comprehend how and why such an atrocity *might have been* committed. They could picture to their imaginations a mode—many modes—and a motive—many motives; and because it was not impossible that either of these numerous modes and motives *could* have been the actual one, they have taken it for granted that one of them *must.* But the ease with which these variable fancies were entertained, and the very plausibility which each assumed, should have been understood as indicative rather of the difficulties than of the facilities which must attend elucidation. I have before observed that it is by prominences above the plane of the ordinary, that reason feels her way, if at all, in her search for the true, and that the proper question in cases such as this, is not so much 'what has occurred?' as 'what has occurred that has never occurred before?' In the investigations at the house of Madame L'Espanaye,* the agents of G—— were discouraged and confounded by that very *unusualness* which, to a properly regulated intellect, would have afforded the surest omen of success; while this same intellect might have been plunged in despair at the ordinary character of all that met the eye in the case of the perfumery-girl, and yet told of nothing but easy triumph to the functionaries of the Prefecture.

"In the case of Madame L'Espanaye and her daughter, there was, even at the beginning of our investigation, no doubt that murder had been committed. The idea of suicide was excluded at once. Here, too, we are freed, at the commencement, from all supposition of self-murder. The body found at the Barrière du Roule, was found under such circumstances as to leave us no room for embarrassment upon this important point. But it has been suggested that the corpse discovered, is not that of the Marie Rogêt for the conviction of whose assassin, or assassins, the reward is offered, and respecting whom, solely, our agreement has been arranged with the Prefect. We both know this gentleman well. It will not do to trust him too

*See "Murders in the Rue Morgue."

far. If, dating our inquiries from the body found, and thence tracing a murderer, we yet discover this body to be that of some other individual than Marie; or, if starting from the living Marie, we find her, yet find her unassassinated—in either case we lose our labor; since it is Monsieur G——with whom we have to deal. For our own purpose, therefore, if not for the purpose of justice, it is indispensable that our first step should be the determination of the identity of the corpse with the Marie Rogêt who is missing.

"With the public the arguments of L'Etoile have had weight; and that the journal itself is convinced of their importance would appear from the manner in which it commences one of its essays upon the subject—'Several of the morning papers of the day,' it says, 'speak of the *conclusive* article in Monday's Etoile.' To me, this article appears conclusive of little beyond the zeal of its inditer. We should bear in mind that, in general, it is the object of our newspapers rather to create a sensation—to make a point—than to further the cause of truth. The latter end is only pursued when it seems coincident with the former. The print which merely falls in with ordinary opinion (however well founded this opinion may be) earns for itself no credit with the mob. The mass of the people regard as profound only him who suggests *pungent contradictions* of the general idea. In ratiocination, not less than in literature, it is the *epigram* which is the most immediately and the most universally appreciated. In both, it is of the lowest order of merit.

"What I mean to say is, that it is the mingled epigram and melodrame of the idea, that Marie Rogêt still lives, rather than any true plausibility in this idea, which have suggested it to L'Etoile, and secured it a favorable reception with the public. Let us examine the heads of this journal's argument; endeavoring to avoid the incoherence with which it is originally set forth.

"The first aim of the writer is to show, from the brevity of the interval between Marie's disappearance and the finding of the floating corpse, that this corpse cannot be that of Marie. The reduction of this interval to its smallest possible dimension, becomes thus, at once, an object with the reasoner. In the rash pursuit of this object, he rushes into mere assumption at the outset. 'It is folly to suppose,' he says, 'that the murder, if murder was committed on her body, could have been consummated soon enough to have enabled

her murderers to throw the body into the river before midnight.'
We demand at once, and very naturally, *why*? Why is it folly to
suppose that the murder was committed *within five minutes* after
the girl's quitting her mother's house? Why is it folly to suppose
that the murder was committed at any given period of the day?
There have been assassinations at all hours. But, had the murder
taken place at any moment between nine o'clock in the morning of
Sunday, and a quarter before midnight, there would still have been
time enough 'to throw the body into the river before midnight.'
This assumption, then, amounts precisely to this—that the murder
was not committed on Sunday at all—and, if we allow L'Etoile to
assume this, we may permit it any liberties whatever. The paragraph
beginning 'It is folly to suppose that the murder, etc.,' however it
appears as printed in L'Etoile, may be imagined to have existed
actually *thus* in the brain of its inditer—'It is folly to suppose that
the murder, if murder was committed on the body, could have been
committed soon enough to have enabled her murderers to throw the
body into the river before midnight; it is folly, we say, to suppose all
this, and to suppose at the same time, (as we are resolved to
suppose,) that the body was *not* thrown in until *after* midnight'—a
sentence sufficiently inconsequential in itself, but not so utterly
preposterous as the one printed.

"Were it my purpose," continued Dupin, "merely to *make out a
case* against this passage of L'Etoile's argument, I might safely leave
it where it is. It is not, however, with L'Etoile that we have to do,
but with the truth. The sentence in question has but one meaning,
as it stands; and this meaning I have fairly stated: but it is material
that we go behind the mere words, for an idea which these words
have obviously intended, and failed to convey. It was the design of
the journalist to say that, at whatever period of the day or night of
Sunday this murder was committed, it was improbable that the
assassins would have ventured to bear the corpse to the river before
midnight. And herein lies, really, the assumption of which I
complain. It is assumed that the murder was committed at such a
position, and under such circumstances, that *the bearing it* to the
river became necessary. Now, the assassination might have taken
place upon the river's brink, or on the river itself; and, thus, the
throwing the corpse in the water might have been resorted to, at

any period of the day or night, as the most obvious and most immediate mode of disposal. You will understand that I suggest nothing here as probable, or as coincident with my own opinion. My design, so far, has no reference to the *facts* of the case. I wish merely to caution you against the whole tone of L'Etoile's *suggestion,* by calling your attention to its *ex parte* character at the outset.

"Having prescribed thus a limit to suit its own preconceived notions; having assumed that, if this were the body of Marie, it could have been in the water but a very brief time; the journal goes on to say:

'All experience has shown that drowned bodies, or bodies thrown into the water immediately after death by violence, require from six to ten days for sufficient decomposition to take place to bring them to the top of the water. Even when a cannon is fired over a corpse, and it rises before at least five or six days' immersion, it sinks again if let alone.'

"These assertions have been tacitly received by every paper in Paris, with the exception of Le Moniteur.* This latter print endeavors to combat that portion of the paragraph which has reference to 'drowned bodies' only, by citing some five or six instances in which the bodies of individuals known to be drowned were found floating after the lapse of less time than is insisted upon by L'Etoile. But there is something excessively unphilosophical in the attempt on the part of Le Moniteur, to rebut the general assertion of L'Etoile, by a citation of particular instances militating against that assertion. Had it been possible to adduce fifty instead of five examples of bodies found floating at the end of two or three days, these fifty examples could still have been properly regarded only as exceptions to L'Etoile's rule, until such time as the rule itself should be confuted. Admitting the rule, (and this Le Moniteur does not deny, insisting merely upon its exceptions,) the argument of L'Etoile is suffered to remain in full force; for this argument does not pretend to involve more than a question of the *probability* of the body having risen to the surface in less than three days; and this probability will be in favor of L'Etoile's position until the instances so childishly adduced shall be sufficient in number to establish an antagonistical rule.

*The "N. Y. Commercial Advertiser," edited by Col. Stone.

"You will see at once that all argument upon this head should be urged, if at all, against the rule itself; and for this end we must examine the *rationale* of the rule. Now the human body, in general, is neither much lighter nor much heavier than the water of the Seine; that is to say, the specific gravity of the human body, in its natural condition, is about equal to the bulk of fresh water which it displaces. The bodies of fat and fleshy persons, with small bones, and of women generally, are lighter than those of the lean and large-boned, and of men; and the specific gravity of the water of a river is somewhat influenced by the presence of the tide from sea. But, leaving this tide out of question, it may be said that *very* few human bodies will sink at all, even in fresh water, *of their own accord.* Almost any one, falling into a river, will be enabled to float, if he suffer the specific gravity of the water fairly to be adduced in comparison with his own—that is to say, if he suffer his whole person to be immersed, with as little exception as possible. The proper position for one who cannot swim, is the upright position of the walker on land, with the head thrown fully back, and immersed; the mouth and nostrils alone remaining above the surface. Thus circumstanced, we shall find that we float without difficulty and without exertion. It is evident, however, that the gravities of the body, and of the bulk of water displaced, are very nicely balanced, and that a trifle will cause either to preponderate. An arm, for instance, uplifted from the water, and thus deprived of its support, is an additional weight sufficient to immerse the whole head, while the accidental aid of the smallest piece of timber will enable us to elevate the head so as to look about. Now, in the struggles of one unused to swimming, the arms are invariably thrown upwards, while an attempt is made to keep the head in its usual perpendicular position. The result is the immersion of the mouth and nostrils, and the inception, during efforts to breathe while beneath the surface, of water into the lungs. Much is also received into the stomach, and the whole body becomes heavier by the difference between the weight of the air originally distending these cavities, and that of the fluid which now fills them. This difference is sufficient to cause the body to sink, as a general rule; but is insufficient in the cases of individuals with small bones and an abnormal quantity of flaccid or fatty matter. Such individuals float even after drowning.

"The corpse, being supposed at the bottom of the river, will there remain until, by some means, its specific gravity again becomes less than that of the bulk of water which it displaces. This effect is brought about by decomposition, or otherwise. The result of decomposition is the generation of gas, distending the cellular tissues and all the cavities, and giving the *puffed* appearance which is so horrible. When this distension has so far progressed that the bulk of the corpse is materially increased without a corresponding increase of *mass* or weight, its specific gravity becomes less than that of the water displaced, and it forthwith makes its appearance at the surface. But decomposition is modified by innumerable circumstances—is hastened or retarded by innumerable agencies; for example, by the heat or cold of the season, by the mineral impregnation or purity of the water, by its depth or shallowness, by its currency or stagnation, by the temperament of the body, by its infection or freedom from disease before death. Thus it is evident that we can assign no period, with any thing like accuracy, at which the corpse shall rise through decomposition. Under certain conditions this result would be brought about within an hour; under others, it might not take place at all. There are chemical infusions by which the animal frame can be preserved *forever* from corruption; the Bi-chloride of Mercury is one. But, apart from decomposition, there may be, and very usually is, a generation of gas within the stomach, from the acetous fermentation of vegetable matter (or within other cavities from other causes) sufficient to induce a distension which will bring the body to the surface. The effect produced by the firing of a cannon is that of simple vibration. This may either loosen the corpse from the soft mud or ooze in which it is imbedded, thus permitting it to rise when other agencies have already prepared it for so doing; or it may overcome the tenacity of some putrescent portions of the cellular tissue; allowing the cavities to distend under the influence of the gas.

"Having thus before us the whole philosophy of this subject, we can easily test by it the assertions of L'Etoile. 'All experience shows,' says this paper, 'that drowned bodies, or bodies thrown into the water immediately after death by violence, require from six to ten days for sufficient decomposition to take place to bring them to the top of the water. Even when a cannon is fired over a corpse, and it rises before at least five or six days' immersion, it sinks again if let alone.'

"The whole of this paragraph must now appear a tissue of inconsequence and incoherence. All experience does *not* show that 'drowned bodies' *require* from six to ten days for sufficient decomposition to take place to bring them to the surface. Both science and experience show that the period of their rising is, and necessarily must be, indeterminate. If, moreover, a body has risen to the surface through firing of cannon, it will *not* 'sink again if let alone,' until decomposition has so far progressed as to permit the escape of the generated gas. But I wish to call your attention to the distinction which is made between 'drowned bodies,' and 'bodies thrown into the water immediately after death by violence.' Although the writer admits the distinction, he yet includes them all in the same category. I have shown how it is that the body of a drowning man becomes specifically heavier than its bulk of water, and that he would not sink at all, except for the struggles by which he elevates his arms above the surface, and his gasps for breath while beneath the surface—gasps which supply by water the place of the original air in the lungs. But these struggles and these gasps would not occur in the body 'thrown into the water immediately after death by violence.' Thus, in the latter instance, *the body, as a general rule, would not sink at all*—a fact of which L'Etoile is evidently ignorant. When decomposition had proceeded to a very great extent—when the flesh had in a great measure left the bones—then, indeed, but not *till* then, should we lose sight of the corpse.

"And now what are we to make of the argument, that the body found could not be that of Marie Rogêt, because, three days only having elapsed, this body was found floating? If drowned, being a woman, she might never have sunk; or having sunk, might have re-appeared in twenty-four hours, or less. But no one supposes her to have been drowned; and, dying before being thrown into the river, she might have been found floating at any period afterwards whatever.

" 'But,' says L'Etoile, 'if the body had been kept in its mangled state on shore until Tuesday night, some trace would be found on shore of the murderers.' Here it is at first difficult to perceive the intention of the reasoner. He means to anticipate what he imagines would be an objection to his theory—viz: that the body was kept on shore two days, suffering rapid decomposition—*more* rapid than if immersed in water. He supposes that, had this been the case, it *might* have appeared at the surface on the Wednesday, and thinks that *only* under such circumstances it could so have appeared. He is accordingly in haste to show that it *was not* kept on shore; for, if so, 'some trace would be found on shore of the murderers.' I presume you smile at the *sequitur*. You cannot be made to see how the mere *duration* of the corpse on the shore could operate to *multiply traces* of the assassins. Nor can I.

" 'And furthermore it is exceedingly improbable,' continues our journal, 'that any villains who had committed such a murder as is here supposed, would have thrown the body in without weight to sink it, when such a precaution could have so easily been taken.' Observe, here, the laughable confusion of thought! No one—not even L'Etoile—disputes the murder committed *on the body found*. The marks of violence are too obvious. It is our reasoner's object merely to show that this body is not Marie's. He wishes to prove that *Marie* is not assassinated—not that the corpse was not. Yet his observation proves only the latter point. Here is a corpse without weight attached. Murderers, casting it in, would not have failed to attach a weight. Therefore it was not thrown in by murderers. This is all which is proved, if any thing is. The question of identity is not even approached, and L'Etoile has been at great pains merely to gainsay now what it has admitted only a moment before. 'We are perfectly convinced,' it says, 'that the body found was that of a murdered female.'

"Nor is this the sole instance, even in this division of his subject, where our reasoner unwittingly reasons against himself. His evident object, I have already said, is to reduce, as much as possible, the interval between Marie's disappearance and the finding of the corpse. Yet we find him *urging* the point that no person saw the girl from the moment of her leaving her mother's house. 'We have no evidence,' he says, 'that Marie Rogêt was in the land of the living

after nine o'clock on Sunday, June the twenty-second.' As his
argument is obviously an *ex parte* one, he should, at least, have left
this matter out of sight; for had any one been known to see Marie,
say on Monday, or on Tuesday, the interval in question would have
been much reduced, and, by his own ratiocination, the probability
much diminished of the corpse being that of the *grisette*. It is,
nevertheless, amusing to observe that L'Etoile insists upon its point
in the full belief of its furthering its general argument.

"Reperuse now that portion of this argument which has reference
to the identification of the corpse by Beauvais. In regard to the *hair*
upon the arm, L'Etoile has been obviously disingenuous.
M. Beauvais, not being an idiot, could never have urged, in
identification of the corpse, simply *hair upon its arm*. No arm is
without hair. The *generality* of the expression of L'Etoile is a mere
perversion of the witness' phraseology. He must have spoken of
some *peculiarity* in this hair. It must have been a peculiarity of
color, of quantity, of length, or of situation.

" 'Her foot,' says the journal, 'was small—so are thousands of feet.
Her garter is no proof whatever—nor is her shoe—for shoes and
garters are sold in packages. The same may be said of the flowers in
her hat. One thing upon which M. Beauvais strongly insists is, that
the clasp on the garter found, had been set back to take it in. This
amounts to nothing; for most women find it proper to take a pair of
garters home and fit them to the size of the limbs they are to
encircle, rather than to try them in the store where they purchase.'
Here it is difficult to suppose the reasoner in earnest. Had
M. Beauvais, in his search for the body of Marie, discovered a corpse
corresponding in general size and appearance to the missing girl, he
would have been warranted (without reference to the question of
habiliment at all) in forming an opinion that his search had been
successful. If, in addition to the point of general size and contour,
he had found upon the arm a peculiar hairy appearance which he
had observed upon the living Marie, his opinion might have been
justly strengthened; and the increase of positiveness might well have
been in the ratio of the peculiarity, or unusualness, of the hairy
mark. If, the feet of Marie being small, those of the corpse were also
small, the increase of probability that the body was that of Marie
would not be an increase in a ratio merely arithmetical, but in one

highly geometrical, or accumulative. Add to all this shoes such as she had been known to wear upon the day of her disappearance, and, although these shoes may be 'sold in packages' you so far augment the probability as to verge upon the certain. What, of itself, would be no evidence of identity, becomes through its corroborative position, proof most sure. Give us, then, flowers in the hat corresponding to those worn by the missing girl, and we seek for nothing farther. If only *one* flower, we seek for nothing farther—what then if two or three, or more? Each successive one is multiple evidence—proof not *added* to proof, but *multiplied* by hundreds or thousands. Let us now discover, upon the deceased, garters such as the living used, and it is almost folly to proceed. But these garters are found to be tightened, by the setting back of a clasp, in just such a manner as her own had been tightened by Marie, shortly previous to her leaving home. It is now madness or hypocrisy to doubt. What L'Etoile says in respect to this abbreviation of the garter's being an usual occurrence, shows nothing beyond its own pertinacity in error. The elastic nature of the clasp-garter is self-demonstration of the *unusualness* of the abbreviation. What is made to adjust itself, must of necessity require foreign adjustment but rarely. It must have been by an accident, in its strictest sense, that these garters of Marie needed the tightening described. They alone would have amply established her identity. But it is not that the corpse was found to have the garters of the missing girl, or found to have her shoes, or her bonnet, or the flowers of her bonnet, or her feet, or a peculiar mark upon the arm, or her general size and appearance—it is that the corpse had each, and *all collectively*. Could it be proved that the editor of L'Etoile *really* entertained a doubt, under the circumstances, there would be no need, in his case, of a commission *de lunatico inquirendo*. He has thought it sagacious to echo the small talk of the lawyers, who, for the most part, content themselves with echoing the rectangular precepts of the courts. I would here observe that very much of what is rejected as evidence by a court, is the best of evidence to the intellect. For the court, guiding itself by the general principles of evidence—the recognized and *booked* principles—is averse from swerving at particular instances. And this steadfast adherence to principle, with rigorous disregard of the conflicting exception, is a

sure mode of attaining the *maximum* of attainable truth, in any
long sequence of time. The practice, *in mass,* is therefore
philosophical; but it is not the less certain that it engenders vast
individual error.*

"In respect to the insinuations levelled at Beauvais, you will be
willing to dismiss them in a breath. You have already fathomed the
true character of this good gentleman. He is a *busy body,* with much
of romance and little of wit. Any one so constituted will readily so
conduct himself, upon occasion of *real* excitement, as to render
himself liable to suspicion on the part of the over-acute, or the ill-
disposed. M. Beauvais (as it appears from your notes) had some
personal interviews with the editor of L'Etoile, and offended him by
venturing an opinion that the corpse, notwithstanding the theory of
the editor, was, in sober fact, that of Marie. 'He persists,' says the
paper, 'in asserting the corpse to be that of Marie, but cannot give a
circumstance, in addition to those which we have commented upon,
to make others believe.' Now, without re-adverting to the fact that
stronger evidence 'to make others believe,' could *never* have been
adduced, it may be remarked that a man may very well be
understood to believe, in a case of this kind, without the ability to
advance a single reason for the belief of a second party. Nothing is
more vague than impressions of individual identity. Each man
recognizes his neighbor, yet there are few instances in which any one
is prepared to *give a reason* for his recognition. The editor of
L'Etoile had no right to be offended at M. Beauvais' unreasoning
belief.

"The suspicious circumstances which invest him, will be found to
tally much better with my hypothesis of *romantic busy-bodyism,*
than with the reasoner's suggestion of guilt. Once adopting the
more charitable interpretation, we shall find no difficulty in
comprehending the rose in the key-hole; the 'Marie' upon the slate;
the 'elbowing the male relatives out of the way;' the 'aversion to

---

*"A theory based on the qualities of an object, will prevent its being unfolded
according to its objects; and he who arranges topics in reference to their causes, will
cease to value them according to their results. Thus the jurisprudence of every nation
will show that, when law becomes a science and a system, it ceases to be justice. The
errors into which a blind devotion to *principles* of classification has led the common
law, will be seen by observing how often the legislature has been obliged to come
forward to restore the equity its scheme had lost."—*Landor.*

permitting them to see the body;' the caution given to Madame
B——, that she must hold no conversation with the *gendarme* until
his return (Beauvais'); and, lastly, his apparent determination 'that
nobody should have anything to do with the proceedings except
himself.' It seems to me unquestionable that Beauvais was a suitor
of Marie's; that she coquetted with him; and that he was ambitious
of being thought to enjoy her fullest intimacy and confidence. I
shall say nothing more upon this point; and, as the evidence fully
rebuts the assertion of L'Etoile, touching the matter of *apathy* on
the part of the mother and other relatives—an apathy inconsistent
with the supposition of their believing the corpse to be that of the
perfumery-girl—we shall now proceed as if the question of *identity*
were settled to our perfect satisfaction."

"And what," I here demanded, "do you think of the opinions of
Le Commerciel?"

"That, in spirit, they are far more worthy of attention than any
which have been promulgated upon the subject. The deductions
from the premises are philosophical and acute; but the premises, in
two instances, at least, are founded in imperfect observation. Le
Commerciel wishes to intimate that Marie was seized by some gang
of low ruffians not far from her mother's door. 'It is impossible,' it
urges, 'that a person so well known to thousands as this young
woman was, should have passed three blocks without some one
having seen her.' This is the idea of a man long resident in Paris—a
public man—and one whose walks to and fro in the city, have been
mostly limited to the vicinity of the public offices. He is aware that
he seldom passes so far as a dozen blocks from his own *bureau,*
without being recognized and accosted. And, knowing the extent of
his personal acquaintance with others, and of others with him, he
compares his notoriety with that of the perfumery-girl, finds no
great difference between them, and reaches at once the conclusion
that she, in her walks, would be equally liable to recognition with
himself in his. This could only be the case were her walks of the
same unvarying, methodical character, and within the same *species*
of limited region as are his own. He passes to and fro, at regular
intervals, within a confined periphery, abounding in individuals
who are led to observation of his person through interest in the
kindred nature of his occupation with their own. But the walks of

Marie may, in general, be supposed discursive. In this particular
instance, it will be understood as most probable, that she proceeded
upon a route of more than average diversity from her accustomed
ones. The parallel which we imagine to have existed in the mind of
Le Commerciel would only be sustained in the event of the two
individuals traversing the whole city. In this case, granting the
personal acquaintances to be equal, the chances would be also equal
that an equal number of personal rencounters would be made. For
my own part, I should hold it not only as possible, but as very far
more than probable, that Marie might have proceeded, at any given
period, by any one of the many routes between her own residence
and that of her aunt, without meeting a single individual whom she
knew, or by whom she was known. In viewing this question in its
full and proper light, we must hold steadily in mind the great
disproportion between the personal acquaintances of even the most
noted individual in Paris, and the entire population of Paris itself.

"But whatever force there may still appear to be in the suggestion
of Le Commerciel, will be much diminished when we take into
consideration *the hour* at which the girl went abroad. 'It was when
the streets were full of people,' says Le Commerciel, 'that she went
out.' But not so. It was at nine o'clock in the morning. Now at nine
o'clock of every morning in the week, *with the exception of Sunday,*
the streets of the city are, it is true, thronged with people. At nine
on Sunday, the populace are chiefly within doors *preparing for
church.* No observing person can have failed to notice the peculiarly
deserted air of the town, from about eight until ten on the morning
of every Sabbath. Between ten and eleven the streets are thronged,
but not at so early a period as that designated.

"There is another point at which there seems a deficiency of
observation on the part of Le Commerciel. 'A piece,' it says, 'of one
of the unfortunate girl's petticoats, two feet long, and one foot wide,
was torn out and tied under her chin, and around the back of her
head, probably to prevent screams. This was done by fellows who
had no pocket-handkerchiefs.' Whether this idea is, or is not well
founded, we will endeavor to see hereafter; but by 'fellows who have
no pocket-handkerchiefs,' the editor intends the lowest class of
ruffians. These, however, are the very description of people who will
always be found to have handkerchiefs even when destitute of shirts.

You must had had occasion to observe how absolutely indispensable, of late years, to the thorough blackguard, has become the pocket-handkerchief.''

"And what are we to think," I asked, "of the article in Le Soleil?''

"That it is a vast pity its inditer was not born a parrot—in which case he would have been the most illustrious parrot of his race. He has merely repeated the individual items of the already published opinion; collecting them, with a laudable industry, from this paper and from that. 'The things had all *evidently* been there,' he says, 'at least, three or four weeks, and there can be *no doubt* that the spot of this appalling outrage has been discovered.' The facts here re-stated by Le Soleil, are very far indeed from removing my own doubts upon this subject, and we will examine them more particularly hereafter in connexion with another division of the theme.

"At present we must occupy ourselves with other investigations. You cannot fail to have remarked the extreme laxity of the examination of the corpse. To be sure, the question of identity was readily determined, or should have been; but there were other points to be ascertained. Had the body been in any respect *despoiled?* Had the deceased any articles of jewelry about her person upon leaving home? if so, had she any when found? These are important questions utterly untouched by the evidence; and there are others of equal moment, which have met with no attention. We must endeavor to satisfy ourselves by personal inquiry. The case of St. Eustache must be re-examined. I have no suspicion of this person; but let us proceed methodically. We will ascertain beyond a doubt the validity of the *affidavits* in regard to his whereabouts on the Sunday. Affidavits of this character are readily made matter of mystification. Should there be nothing wrong here, however, we will dismiss St. Eustache from our investigations. His suicide, however corroborative of suspicion, were there found to be deceit in the affidavits, is, without such deceit, in no respect an unaccountable circumstance, or one which need cause us to deflect from the line of ordinary analysis.

"In that which I now propose, we will discard the interior points of this tragedy, and concentrate our attention upon its outskirts. Not the least usual error, in investigations such as this, is the limiting of inquiry to the immediate, with total disregard of the collateral or circumstantial events. It is the mal-practice of the courts to confine evidence and discussion to the bounds of apparent relevancy. Yet experience has shown, and a true philosophy will always show, that a vast, perhaps the larger portion of truth, arises from the seemingly irrelevant. It is through the spirit of this principle, if not precisely through its letter, that modern science has resolved to *calculate upon the unforeseen*. But perhaps you do not comprehend me. The history of human knowledge has so uninterruptedly shown that to collateral, or incidental, or accidental events we are indebted for the most numerous and most valuable discoveries, that it has at length become necessary, in any prospective view of improvement, to make not only large, but the largest allowances for inventions that shall arise by chance, and quite out of the range of ordinary expectation. It is no longer philosophical to base, upon what has been, a vision of what is to be. *Accident* is admitted as a portion of the substructure. We make chance a matter of absolute calculation. We subject the unlooked for and unimagined, to the mathematical *formulae* of the schools.

"I repeat that it is no more than fact, that the *larger* portion of all truth has sprung from the collateral; and it is but in accordance with the spirit of the principle involved in this fact, that I would divert inquiry, in the present case, from the trodden and hitherto unfruitful ground of the event itself, to the contemporary circumstances which surround it. While you ascertain the validity of the affidavits, I will examine the newspapers more generally than you have as yet done. So far, we have only reconnoitred the field of investigation; but it will be strange indeed if a comprehensive survey, such as I propose, of the public prints, will not afford us some minute points which shall establish a *direction* for inquiry."

In pursuance of Dupin's suggestion, I made scrupulous examination of the affair of the affidavits. The result was a firm conviction of their validity, and of the consequent innocence of St. Eustache. In the mean time my friend occupied himself, with what seemed to me a minuteness altogether objectless, in a scrutiny of the various newspaper files. At the end of a week he placed before me the following extracts:

"About three years and a half ago, a disturbance very similar to the present, was caused by the disappearance of this same Marie Rogêt, from the *parfumerie* of Monsieur Le Blanc, in the Palais Royal. At the end of a week, however, she re-appeared at her customary *comptoir,* as well as ever, with the exception of a slight paleness not altogether usual. It was given out by Monsieur Le Blanc and her mother, that she had merely been on a visit to some friend in the country; and the affair was speedily hushed up. We presume that the present absence is a freak of the same nature, and that, at the expiration of a week, or perhaps of a month, we shall have her among us again."—*Evening Paper—Monday, June 23.**

"An evening journal of yesterday, refers to a former mysterious disappearance of Mademoiselle Rogêt. It is well known that, during the week of her absence from Le Blanc's *parfumerie,* she was in the company of a young naval officer, much noted for his debaucheries. A quarrel, it is supposed, providentially led to her return home. We have the name of the Lothario in question, who is, at present, stationed in Paris, but, for obvious reasons, forbear to make it public."—*Le Mercurie—Tuesday Morning, June 24.†*

"An outrage of the most atrocious character was perpetrated near this city the day before yesterday. A gentleman, with his wife and daughter, engaged, about dusk, the services of six young men, who were idly rowing a boat to and fro near the banks of the Seine, to convey him across the river. Upon reaching the opposite shore, the three passengers stepped out, and had proceeded so far as to be beyond the view of the boat, when the daughter discovered that she had left in it her parasol. She returned for it, was seized by the gang, carried out into the stream, gagged, brutally treated, and finally taken to the shore at a point not far from that at which she had originally entered the boat with her parents. The villains have escaped for the time, but the police are upon their trail, and some of them will soon be taken."—*Morning Paper—June 25.‡*

"We have received one or two communications, the object of which is to fasten the crime of the late atrocity upon Mennais;§ but as this gentleman has been fully exonerated by a legal inquiry, and as the arguments of our several correspondents appear to be more zealous than profound, we do not think it advisable to make them public."—*Morning Paper—June 28.‡*

"We have received several forcibly written communications, apparently from various sources, and which go far to render it a matter of certainty that the unfortunate Marie Rogêt has become a victim of one of the numerous bands of blackguards which infest the vicinity of the city upon Sunday. Our own opinion is decidedly in favor of this supposition. We

*"N. Y. Express."
†"N. Y. Herald."
‡"N. Y. Courier and Inquirer."
§Mennais was one of the parties originally suspected and arrested, but discharged through total lack of evidence.

shall endeavor to make room for some of these arguments
hereafter."—*Evening Paper—Tuesday, June* 31.*

"On Monday, one of the bargemen connected with the revenue service,
saw an empty boat floating down the Seine. Sails were lying in the bottom of
the boat. The bargeman towed it under the barge office. The next morning
it was taken from thence, without the knowledge of any of the officers. The
rudder is now at the barge office." —*Le Diligence—Thursday, June* 26.†

Upon reading these various extracts, they not only seemed to me
irrelevant, but I could perceive no mode in which any one of them
could be brought to bear upon the matter in hand. I waited for
some explanation from Dupin.

"It is not my present design," he said, "to *dwell* upon the first and
second of these extracts. I have copied them chiefly to show you the
extreme remissness of the police, who, as far as I can understand
from the Prefect, have not troubled themselves, in any respect, with
an examination of the naval officer alluded to. Yet it is mere folly to
say that between the first and second disappearance of Marie, there
is no *supposable* connection. Let us admit the first elopement to
have resulted in a quarrel between the lovers, and the return home
of the betrayed. We are now prepared to view a second *elopement*
(if we *know* that an elopement has again taken place) as indicating
a renewal of the betrayer's advances, rather than as the result of new
proposals by a second individual—we are prepared to regard it as a
'making up' of the old *amour,* rather than as the commencement of
a new one. The chances are ten to one, that he who had once eloped
with Marie, would again propose an elopement, rather than that she
to whom proposals of elopement had been made by one individual,
should have them made to her by another. And here let me call
your attention to the fact, that the time elapsing between the first
ascertained, and the second supposed elopement, is a few months
more than the general period of the cruises of our men-of-war. Had
the lover been interrupted in his first villany by the necessity of
departure to sea, and had he seized the first moment of his return to
renew the base designs not yet altogether accomplished—or not yet
altogether accomplished *by him?* Of all these things we know
nothing.

"You will say, however, that, in the second instance, there was *no*

*"N. Y. Evening Post."
†"N. Y. Standard."

elopement as imagined. Certainly not—but are we prepared to say that there was not the frustrated design? Beyond St. Eustache, and perhaps Beauvais, we find no recognized, no open, no honorable suitors of Marie. Of none other is there any thing said. Who, then, is the secret lover, of whom the relatives *(at least most of them)* know nothing, but whom Marie meets upon the morning of Sunday, and who is so deeply in her confidence, that she hesitates not to remain with him until the shades of the evening descend, amid the solitary groves of the Barrière du Roule? Who is that secret lover, I ask, of whom, at least, *most* of the relatives know nothing? And what means the singular prophecy of Madame Rogêt on the morning of Marie's departure?—'I fear that I shall never see Marie again.'

"But if we cannot imagine Madame Rogêt privy to the design of elopement, may we not at least suppose this design entertained by the girl? Upon quitting home, she gave it to be understood that she was about to visit her aunt in the Rue des Drômes, and St. Eustache was requested to call for her at dark. Now at first glance, this fact strongly militates against my suggestion;—but let us reflect. That she *did* meet some companion, and proceed with him across the river, reaching the Barrière du Roule at so late an hour as three o'clock in the afternoon, is known. But in consenting so to accompany this individual, **(for whatever purpose—to her mother known or unknown,)*** she must have thought of her expressed intention when leaving home, and of the surprise and suspicion aroused in the bosom of her affianced suitor, St. Eustache, when, calling for her, at the hour appointed, in the Rue des Drômes, he should find that she had not been there, and when, moreover, upon returning to the *pension* with this alarming intelligence, he should become aware of her continued absence from home. She must have thought of these things, I say. She must have foreseen the chagrin of St. Eustache, the suspicion of all. She could not have thought of returning to brave this suspicion; but the suspicion becomes a point of trivial importance to her, if we suppose her *not* intending to return.

"We may imagine her thinking thus—'I am to meet a certain person for the purpose of elopement, **or for certain other purposes**

[*Boldface type indicates Poe's changes—additions and deletions. The material he deleted is in brackets [**thus**].]

known only to myself. It is necessary that there be no chance of interruption—there must be sufficient time given us to elude pursuit—I will give it to be understood that I shall visit and spend the day with my aunt at the Rue des Drômes—I will tell St. Eustache not to call for me until dark—in this way, my absence from home for the longest possible period, without causing suspicion or anxiety, will be accounted for, and I shall gain more time than in any other manner. If I bid St. Eustache call for me at dark, he will be sure not to call before; but, if I wholly neglect to bid him call, my time for escape will be diminished, since it will be expected that I return the earlier, and my absence will the sooner excite anxiety. Now, if it were my design to return *at all*—if I had in contemplation merely a stroll with the individual in question—it would not be my policy to bid St. Eustache call; for, calling, he will be *sure* to ascertain that I have played him false—a fact of which I might keep him for ever in ignorance, by leaving home without notifying him of my intention, by returning before dark, and by then stating that I had been to visit my aunt in the Rue des Drômes. But, as it is my design *never* to return—**or not for some weeks—or not until certain concealments are effected**—the gaining of time is the only point about which I need give myself any concern.'

"You have observed, in your notes, that the most general opinion in relation to this sad affair is, and was from the first, that the girl had been the victim of *a gang* of blackguards. Now, the popular opinion, under certain conditions, is not to be disregarded. When arising of itself—when manifesting itself in a strictly spontaneous manner—we should look upon it as analogous with that *intuition* which is the idiosyncrasy of the individual man of genius. In ninety-nine cases from the hundred I would abide by its decision. But it is important that we find no palpable traces of *suggestion*. The opinion must be rigorously *the public's own;* and the distinction is often exceedingly difficult to perceive and to maintain. In the present instance, it appears to me that this 'public opinion,' in respect to *a gang,* has been superinduced by the collateral event which is detailed in the third of my extracts. All Paris is excited by the discovered corpse of Marie, a girl young, beautiful and notorious. This corpse is found, bearing marks of violence, and floating in the river. But it is now made known that, at the very

period, or about the very period, in which it is supposed that the
girl was assassinated, an outrage similar in nature to that endured by
the deceased, although less in extent, was perpetrated, by a gang of
young ruffians, upon the person of a second young female. Is it
wonderful that the one known atrocity should influence the popular
judgment in regard to the other unknown? This judgment awaited
direction, and the known outrage seemed so opportunely to afford
it! Marie, too, was found in the river; and upon this very river was
this known outrage committed. The connexion of the two events
had about it so much of the palpable, that the true wonder would
have been a *failure* of the populace to appreciate and to seize it.
But, in fact, the one atrocity, known to be so committed, is, if any
thing, evidence that the other, committed at a time nearly
coincident, was *not* so committed. It would have been a miracle
indeed, if, while a gang of ruffians were perpetrating, at a given
locality, a most unheard-of wrong, there should have been another
similar gang, in a similar locality, in the same city, under the same
circumstances, with the same means and appliances, engaged in a
wrong of precisely the same aspect, at precisely the same period of
time! Yet in what, if not in this marvellous train of coincidence,
does the accidentally *suggested* opinion of the populace call upon us
to believe?

"Before proceeding farther, let us consider the supposed scene of
the assassination, in the thicket at the Barrière du Roule. This
thicket, although dense, was in the close vicinity of a public road.
Within were three or four large stones, forming a kind of seat with a
back and footstool. On the upper stone was discovered a white
petticoat; on the second, a silk scarf. A parasol, gloves, and a pocket-
handkerchief, were also here found. The handkerchief bore the
name, 'Marie Rogêt.' Fragments of dress were seen on the branches
around. The earth was trampled, the bushes were broken, and there
was every evidence of a violent struggle.

"Notwithstanding the acclamation with which the discovery of
this thicket was received by the press, and the unanimity with which
it was supposed to indicate the precise scene of the outrage, it must
be admitted that there was some very good reason for doubt. That it
was the scene, I **may or I may not** believe—but there was excellent
reason for doubt. Had the *true* scene been, as Le Commerciel

suggested, in the neighborhood of the Rue Pavée St. Andrée, the perpetrators of the crime, supposing them still resident in Paris, would naturally have been stricken with terror at the public attention thus acutely directed into the proper channel; and, in certain classes of minds, there would have arisen, at once, a sense of the necessity of some exertion to redivert this attention. And thus, the thicket of the Barrière du Roule having been already suspected, the idea of placing the articles where they were found, might have been naturally entertained. There is no real evidence, although Le Soleil so supposes, that the articles discovered had been more than a very few days in the thicket; while there is much circumstantial proof that they could not have remained there, without attracting attention, during the twenty days elapsing between the fatal Sunday and the afternoon upon which they were found by the boys. 'They were all *mildewed* down hard,' says Le Soleil, adopting the opinions of its predecessors, 'with the action of the rain, and stuck together from *mildew*. The grass had grown around and over some of them. The silk of the parasol was strong, but the threads of it were run together within. The upper part, where it had been doubled and folded, was all *mildewed* and rotten, and tore on being opened.' In respect to the grass having 'grown around and over some of them,' it is obvious that the fact could only have been ascertained from the words, and thus from the recollections, of two small boys; for these boys removed the articles and took them home before they had been seen by a third party. But grass will grow, especially in warm and damp weather, (such as was that of the period of the murder,) as much as two or three inches in a single day. A parasol lying upon a newly turfed ground, might, in a single week, be entirely concealed from sight by the upspringing grass. And touching that *mildew* upon which the editor of Le Soleil so pertinaciously insists, that he employs the word no less than three times in the brief paragraph just quoted, is he really unaware of the nature of this *mildew*? Is he to be told that it is one of the many classes of *fungus*, of which the most ordinary feature is its upspringing and decadence within twenty-four hours?

"Thus we see, at a glance, that what has been most triumphantly adduced in support of the idea that the articles had been 'for at least three or four weeks' in the thicket, is most absurdly null as regards any evidence of that fact. On the other hand, it is exceedingly difficult to believe that these articles could have remained in the thicket specified, for a longer period than a single week—for a longer period than from one Sunday to the next. Those who know any thing of the vicinity of Paris, know the extreme difficulty of finding *seclusion,* unless at a great distance from its suburbs. Such a thing as an unexplored, or even an unfrequently visited recess, amid its woods or groves, is not for a moment to be imagined. Let any one who, being at heart a lover of nature, is yet chained by duty to the dust and heat of this great metropolis—let any such one attempt, even during the week-days, to slake his thirst for solitude amid the scenes of natural loveliness which immediately surround us. At every second step, he will find the growing charm dispelled by the voice and personal intrusion of some ruffian or party of carousing blackguards. He will seek privacy amid the densest foliage, all in vain. Here are the very nooks where the unwashed most abound—here are the temples most desecrate. With sickness of the heart the wanderer will flee back to the polluted Paris as to a less odious because less incongruous sink of pollution. But if the vicinity of the city is so beset during the working days of the week, how much more so on the Sabbath! It is now especially that, released from the claims of labor, or deprived of the customary opportunities of crime, the town blackguard seeks the precincts of the town, not through love of the rural, which in his heart he despises, but by way of escape from the restraints and conventionalities of society. He desires less the fresh air and the green trees, than the utter *license* of the country. Here, at the road-side inn, or beneath the foliage of the woods, he indulges, unchecked by any eye except those of his boon companions, in all the mad excess of a counterfeit hilarity—the joint offspring of liberty and of rum. I say nothing more than what must be obvious to every dispassionate observer, when I repeat that the circumstance of the articles in question having remained undiscovered, for a longer period than from one Sunday to another, in *any* thicket in the immediate neighborhood of Paris, is to be looked upon as little less than miraculous.

"But there are not wanting other grounds for the suspicion that the articles were placed in the thicket with the view of diverting attention from the real scene of the outrage. And, first, let me direct your notice to the *date* of the discovery of the articles. Collate this with the date of the fifth extract made by myself from the newspapers. You will find that the discovery followed, almost immediately, the urgent communications sent to the evening paper. These communications, although various, and apparently from various sources, tended all to the same point—viz., the directing of attention to *a gang* as the perpetrators of the outrage, and to the neighborhood of the Barrière du Roule as its scene. Now here, of course, the suspicion is not that, in consequence of these communications, or of the public attention by them directed, the articles were found by the boys; but the suspicion might and may well have been, that the articles were not *before* found by the boys, for the reason that the articles had not before been in the thicket; having been deposited there only at so late a period as at the date, or shortly prior to the date of the communications, by the guilty authors of these communications themselves.

"This thicket was a singular—an exceedingly singular one. It was unusually dense. Within its naturally walled enclosure were three extraordinary stones, *forming a seat with a back and footstool.* And this thicket, so full of a natural art, was in the immediate vicinity, *within a few rods,* of the dwelling of Madame Deluc, whose boys were in the habit of closely examining the shrubberies about them in search of the bark of the sassafras. Would it be a rash wager—a wager of one thousand to one—that *a day* never passed over the heads of these boys without finding at least one of them ensconced in the umbrageous hall, and enthroned upon its natural throne? Those who would hesitate at such a wager, have either never been boys themselves, or have forgotten the boyish nature. I repeat—it is exceedingly hard to comprehend how the articles could have remained in this thicket undiscovered, for a longer period than one or two days; and that thus there is good ground for suspicion, in spite of the dogmatic ignorance of Le Soleil, that they were, at a comparatively late date, deposited where found.

"But there are still other and stronger reasons for believing them so deposited, than any which I have as yet urged. And, now, let me beg your notice to the highly artificial arrangement of the articles. On the *upper* stone lay a white petticoat; on the *second* a silk scarf;

scattered around, were a parasol, gloves, and a pocket-handkerchief
bearing the name, 'Marie Rogêt.' Here is just such an arrangement
as would *naturally* be made by a not-over-acute person wishing to
dispose the articles *naturally*. But it is by no means a *really* natural
arrangement. I should rather have looked to see the things *all* lying
on the ground and trampled under foot. In the narrow limits of that
bower, it would have been scarcely possible that the petticoat and
scarf should have retained a position upon the stones, when
subjected to the brushing to and fro of many struggling persons.
'There was evidence,' it is said, 'of a struggle; and the earth was
trampled, the bushes were broken,'—but the petticoat and the scarf
are found deposited as if upon shelves. 'The pieces of the frock torn
out by the bushes were about three inches wide and six inches long.
One part was the hem of the frock and it had been mended. They
looked like strips torn off.' Here, inadvertently, Le Soleil has
employed an exceedingly suspicious phrase. The pieces, as described,
do indeed 'look like strips torn off;' but purposely and by hand. It is
one of the rarest of accidents that a piece is 'torn off,' from any
garment such as is now in question, by the agency *of a thorn*. From
the very nature of such fabrics, a thorn or nail becoming entangled
in them, tears them rectangularly—divides them into two
longitudinal rents, at right angles with each other, and meeting at
an apex where the thorn enters—but it is scarcely possible to
conceive the piece 'torn off.' I never so knew it, nor did you. To
tear a piece *off* from such fabric, two distinct forces, in different
directions, will be, in almost every case, required. If there be two
edges to the fabric—if, for example, it be a pocket-handkerchief, and
it is desired to tear from it a slip, then, and then only, will the one
force serve the purpose. But in the present case the question is of a
dress, presenting but one edge. To tear a piece from the interior,
where no edge is presented, could only be effected by a miracle
through the agency of thorns, and no *one* thorn could accomplish it.
But, even where an edge is presented, two thorns will be necessary,
operating, the one in two distinct directions, and the other in one.
And this in the supposition that the edge is unhemmed. If hemmed,
the matter is nearly out of the question. We thus see the numerous
and great obstacles in the way of pieces being 'torn off' through the
simple agency of 'thorns;' yet we are required to believe not only

that one piece but that many have been so torn. 'And one part,' too, *'was the hem of the frock!'* Another piece was *'part of the skirt, not the hem,'*—that is to say, was torn completely out, through the agency of thorns, from the unedged interior of the dress! These, I say, are things which one may well be pardoned for disbelieving; yet, taken collectedly, they form, perhaps, less of reasonable ground for suspicion, than the one startling circumstance of the articles' having been left in this thicket at all, by any *murderers* who had enough precaution to think of removing the corpse. You will not have apprehended me rightly, however, if you suppose it my design to *deny* this thicket as the scene of the outrage. **There might have been a wrong here, or, more possibly, an accident at Madame Deluc's.** But, in fact, this is a point of minor importance. We are not engaged in an attempt to discover the scene, but to produce the perpetrators of the murder. What I have adduced, notwithstanding the minuteness with which I have adduced it, has been with the view, first, to show the folly of the positive and headlong assertions of Le Soleil, but secondly and chiefly, to bring you, by the most natural route, to a further contemplation of the doubt whether this assassination has, or has not been, the work of *a gang.*

"We will resume this question by mere allusion to the revolting details of the surgeon examined at the inquest. It is only necessary to say that his published *inferences,* in regard to the number of the ruffians, have been properly ridiculed as unjust and totally baseless, by all the reputable anatomists of Paris. Not that the matter *might not* have been as inferred, but that there was no ground for the inference:—**was there not much for another?**

"Let us reflect now upon 'the traces of a struggle;' and let me ask what these traces have been supposed to demonstrate. A gang. But do they not rather demonstrate the absence of a gang? What *struggle* could have taken place—what struggle so violent and so enduring as to have left its 'traces' in all directions—between a weak and defenceless girl and the *gang* of ruffians imagined? The silent grasp of a few rough arms and all would have been over. The victim must have been absolutely passive at their will. You will here bear in mind that [**I admit the thicket as the scene of the outrage; and you will immediately perceive that**] the arguments urged against the thicket as the scene, are applicable, in chief part, only against it as the scene of an outrage committed by *more than a single individual*. If we imagine but *one* violator, we can conceive, and thus only conceive, the struggle of so violent and so obstinate a nature as to have left the 'traces' apparent.

"And again. I have already mentioned the suspicion to be excited by the fact that the articles in question were suffered to remain *at all* in the thicket where discovered. It seems almost impossible that these evidences of guilt should have been accidentally left where found. There was sufficient presence of mind (it is supposed) to remove the corpse; and yet a more positive evidence than the corpse itself (whose features might have been quickly obliterated by decay,) is allowed to lie conspicuously in the scene of the outrage—I allude to the handkerchief with the *name* of the deceased. If this was accident, it was not the accident *of a gang*. We can imagine it only the accident of an individual. Let us see. An individual has committed the murder. He is alone with the ghost of the departed. He is appalled by what lies motionless before him. The fury of his passion is over, and there is abundant room in his heart for the natural awe of the deed. His is none of that confidence which the presence of numbers inevitably inspires. He is *alone* with the dead. He trembles and is bewildered. Yet there is a necessity for disposing of the corpse. He bears it to the river, but leaves behind him the other evidences of guilt; for it is difficult, if not impossible to carry all the burthen at once, and it will be easy to return for what is left. But in his toilsome journey to the water his fears redouble within him. The sounds of life encompass his path. A dozen times he hears or fancies the step of an observer. Even the very lights from the city bewilder him. Yet, in time, and by long and frequent pauses of deep agony, he reaches the river's brink, and disposes of his ghastly charge—perhaps through the medium of a boat. But *now* what treasure does the world hold—what threat of vengeance could it hold out—which would have power to urge the return of that lonely murderer over that toilsome and perilous path, to the thicket and its blood-chilling recollections? He returns *not,* let the consequences be what they may. He *could* not return if he would. His sole thought is immediate escape. He turns his back *forever* upon those dreadful shrubberies, and flees as from the wrath to come.

"But how with a gang? Their number would have inspired them

with confidence; if, indeed, confidence is ever wanting in the breast
of the arrant blackguard; and of arrant blackguards alone are the
supposed *gangs* ever constituted. Their number, I say, would have
prevented the bewildering and unreasoning terror which I have
imagined to paralyze the single man. Could we suppose an oversight
in one, or two, or three, this oversight would have been remedied by
a fourth. They would have left nothing behind them; for their
number would have enabled them to carry *all* at once. There would
have been no need of *return*.

"Consider now the circumstance that, in the outer garment of the
corpse when found, 'a slip, about a foot wide, had been torn upward
from the bottom hem to the waist, wound three times round the
waist, and secured by a sort of hitch in the back.' This was done
with the obvious design of affording *a handle* by which to carry the
body. But would any *number* of men have dreamed of resorting to
such an expedient? To three or four, the limbs of the corpse would
have afforded not only a sufficient, but the best possible hold. The
device is that of a single individual; and this brings us to the fact
that 'between the thicket and the river, the rails of the fences were
found taken down, and the ground bore evident traces of some
heavy burden having been dragged along it!' But would a *number*
of men have put themselves to the superfluous trouble of taking
down a fence, for the purpose of dragging through it a corpse which
they might have *lifted over* any fence in an instant? Would a
number of men have so *dragged* a corpse at all as to have left
evident *traces* of the dragging?

"And here we must refer to an observation of Le Commerciel; an
observation upon which I have already, in some measure,
commented. 'A piece,' says this journal, 'of one of the unfortunate
girl's petticoats was torn out and tied under her chin, and around
the back of her head, probably to prevent screams. This was done by
fellows who had no pocket-handkerchiefs.'

"I have before suggested that a genuine blackguard is never
without a pocket-handkerchief. But it is not to this fact that I now
especially advert. That it was not through want of a handkerchief
for the purpose imagined by Le Commerciel, that this bandage was
employed, is rendered apparent by the handkerchief left in the
thicket; and that the object was not 'to prevent screams' appears,

also, from the bandage having been employed in preference to what
would so much better have answered the purpose. But the language
of the evidence speaks of the strip in question as 'found around the
neck, fitting loosely, and secured with a hard knot.' These words are
sufficiently vague, but differ materially from those of Le
Commerciel. The slip was eighteen inches wide, and therefore,
although of muslin, would form a strong band when folded or
rumpled longitudinally. And thus rumpled it was discovered. My
inference is this. The solitary murderer, having borne the corpse,
for some distance, **(whether from the thicket or elsewhere)** by
means of the bandage *hitched* around its middle, found the weight,
in this mode of procedure, too much for his strength. He resolved to
drag the burthen—the evidence goes to show that it *was* dragged.
With this object in view, it became necessary to attach something
like a rope to one of the extremities. It could be best attached about
the neck, where the head would prevent its slipping off. And, now,
the murderer bethought him, unquestionably, of the bandage about
the loins. He would have used this, but for its volution about the
corpse, the *hitch* which embarrassed it, and the reflection that it had
not been 'torn off' from the garment. It was easier to tear a new slip
from the petticoat. He tore it, made it fast about the neck, and so
dragged his victim to the brink of the river. That this 'bandage,'
only attainable with trouble and delay, and but imperfectly
answering its purpose—that this bandage was employed *at all,*
demonstrates that the necessity for its employment sprang from
circumstances arising at a period when the handkerchief was no
longer attainable—that is to say, arising, as we have imagined, after
quitting the thicket, **(if the thicket it was)**, and on the road
between the thicket and the river.

"But the evidence, you will say, of Madame Deluc, (!) points
especially to the presence of *a gang,* in the vicinity of the thicket, at
or about the epoch of the murder. This I grant. I doubt if there
were not a *dozen* gangs, such as described by Madame Deluc, in and
about the vicinity of the Barrière du Roule at *or about* the period
of this tragedy. But the gang which has drawn upon itself the
pointed animadversion, although the somewhat tardy **and very
suspicious** evidence of Madame Deluc, is the *only* gang which is
represented by that honest and scrupulous old lady as having eaten

her cakes and swallowed her brandy, without putting themselves to the trouble of making her payment. *Et hinc illæ iræ?*

"But what *is* the precise evidence of Madame Deluc? 'A gang of miscreants made their appearance, behaved boisterously, ate and drank without making payment, followed in the route of the young man and girl, returned to the inn *about dusk,* and recrossed the river as if in great haste.'

"Now this 'great haste' very possibly seemed *greater* haste in the eyes of Madame Deluc, since she dwelt lingeringly and lamentingly upon her violated cakes and ale—cakes and ale for which she might still have entertained a faint hope of compensation. Why, otherwise, since it was *about dusk,* should she make a point of the *haste?* It is no cause for wonder, surely, that even a gang of blackguards should make *haste* to get home, when a wide river is to be crossed in small boats, when storm impends, and when night *approaches.*

"I say *approaches;* for the night had *not yet arrived.* It was only *about dusk* that the indecent haste of these 'miscreants' offended the sober eyes of Madame Deluc. But we are told that it was upon this very evening that Madame Deluc, as well as her eldest son, 'heard the screams of a female in the vicinity of the inn.' And in what words does Madame Deluc designate the period of the evening at which these screams were heard? 'It was *soon after dark,*' she says. But 'soon *after* dark,' is, at least, *dark;* and 'about dusk' is as certainly daylight. Thus it is abundantly clear that the gang quitted the Barrière du Roule *prior* to the screams overheard (?) by Madame Deluc. And although, in all the many reports of the evidence, the relative expressions in question are distinctly and invariably employed just as I have employed them in this conversation with yourself, no notice whatever of the gross discrepancy has, as yet, been taken by any of the public journals, or by any of the Myrmidons of police.

"I shall add but one to the arguments against *a gang;* but this *one* has, to my own understanding at least, a weight altogether irresistible. Under the circumstances of large reward offered, and full pardon to any King's evidence, it is not to be imagined, for a moment, that some member of *a gang* of low ruffians, or of any body of men, would not long ago have betrayed his accomplices. Each one of a gang so placed, is not so much greedy of reward, or anxious for escape, as *fearful of betrayal*. He betrays eagerly and early that *he may not himself be betrayed*. That the secret has not been divulged, is the very best of proof that it is, in fact, a secret. The horrors of this dark deed are known only to *one,* **or two,** living human beings, and to God.

"Let us sum up now the meagre yet certain fruits of our long analysis. We have attained the idea **either of a fatal accident under the roof of Madame Deluc, or** of a murder perpetrated, in the thicket at the Barrière du Roule, by a lover, or at least by an intimate and secret associate of the deceased. This associate is of swarthy complexion. This complexion, the 'hitch' in the bandage, and the 'sailor's knot,' with which the bonnet-ribbon is tied, point to a seaman. His companionship with the deceased, a gay, but not an abject young girl, designates him as above the grade of the common sailor. Here the well written and urgent communications to the journals are much in the way of corroboration. The circumstance of the first elopement, as mentioned by Le Mercurie, tends to blend the idea of this seaman with that of the 'naval officer' who is first known to have led the unfortunate into crime. [**We are not forced to suppose a premeditated design of murder or of violation. But there was the friendly shelter of the thicket, and the approach of rain—there was opportunity and strong temptation—and then a sudden and violent wrong, to be concealed only by one of darker dye.**]

"And here, most fitly, comes the consideration of the continued absence of him of the dark complexion. Let me pause to observe that the complexion of this man is dark and swarthy; it was no common swarthiness which constituted the *sole* point of remembrance, both as regards Valence and Madame Deluc. But why is this man absent? Was he murdered by the gang? If so, why are there only *traces* of the assassinated *girl?* The scene of the two outrages will naturally be supposed identical. And where is his corpse? The assassins would most probably have disposed of both in the same way. But it may be said that this man lives, and is deterred from making himself known, through dread of being charged with the murder. This consideration might be supposed to operate upon him now—at this late period—since it has been given in evidence that he was seen with Marie—but it would have had no force at the period of the deed. The first impulse of an innocent man would have been to announce the outrage, and to aid in identifying the ruffians. This *policy* would have suggested. He had been seen with the girl. He had crossed the river with her in an open ferry-boat. The denouncing of the assassins would have appeared, even to an idiot, the surest and sole means of relieving himself from suspicion. We cannot suppose him, on the night of the fatal Sunday, both innocent himself and incognizant of an outrage committed. Yet only under such circumstances is it possible to imagine that he would have failed, if alive, in the denouncement of the assassins.

"And what means are ours, of attaining the truth? We shall find these means multiplying and gathering distinctness as we proceed. Let us sift to the bottom this affair of the first elopement. Let us know the full history of 'the officer,' with his present circumstances, and his whereabouts at the precise period of the murder. Let us carefully compare with each other the various communications sent to the evening paper, in which the object was to inculpate *a gang*. This done, let us compare these communications, both as regards style and MS., with those sent to the morning paper, at a previous period, and insisting so vehemently upon the guilt of Mennais. And, all this done, let us again compare these various communications with the known MSS. of the officer. Let us endeavor to ascertain, by repeated questionings of Madame Deluc and her boys, as well as of the omnibus-driver, Valence, something more of the personal appearance and bearing of the 'man of dark complexion.' Queries, skilfully directed, will not fail to elicit, from some of these parties, information on this particular point (**or upon others**)—information which the parties themselves may not even be aware of possessing. And let us now trace *the boat* picked up by the bargeman on the morning of Monday the twenty-third of June, and which was removed from the barge-office, without the cognizance of the officer in attendance, and *without the rudder,* at some period prior to the discovery of the corpse. With a proper caution and perseverance we shall infallibly trace this boat; for not only can the bargeman who picked it up identify it, but the *rudder is at hand.* The rudder *of a sail-boat* would not have been abandoned, without inquiry, by one altogether at ease in heart. And here let me pause to insinuate a question. There was no *advertisement* of the picking up of this boat.

It was silently taken to the barge-office, and as silently removed. But its owner or employer—how *happened* he, at so early a period as Tuesday morning, to be informed, without the agency of advertisement, of the locality of the boat taken up on Monday, unless we imagine some connexion with the *navy*—some personal permanent connexion leading to cognizance of its minute interests—its petty local news?

"In speaking of the lonely assassin dragging his burden to the shore, I have already suggested the probability of his availing himself *of a boat*. Now we are to understand that Marie Rogêt *was* precipitated from a boat. This would naturally have been the case. The corpse could not have been trusted to the shallow waters of the shore. The peculiar marks on the back and shoulders of the victim tell of the bottom ribs of a boat. That the body was found without weight is also corroborative of the idea. If thrown from the shore a weight would have been attached. We can only account for its absence by supposing the murderer to have neglected the precaution of supplying himself with it before pushing off. In the act of consigning the corpse to the water, he would unquestionably have noticed his oversight; but then no remedy would have been at hand. Any risk would have been preferred to a return to that accursed shore. Having rid himself of his ghastly charge, the murderer would have hastened to the city. There, at some obscure wharf, he would have leaped on land. But the boat—would he have secured it? He would have been in too great haste for such things as securing a boat. Moreover, in fastening it to the wharf, he would have felt as if securing evidence against himself. His natural thought would have been to cast from him, as far as possible, all that had held connection with his crime. He would not only have fled from the wharf, but he would not have permitted *the boat* to remain. Assuredly he would have cast it adrift. Let us pursue our fancies.—In the morning, the wretch is stricken with unutterable horror at finding that the boat has been picked up and detained at a locality which he is in the daily habit of frequenting—at a locality, perhaps, which his duty compels him to frequent. The next night, *without daring to ask for the rudder*, he removes it. Now *where* is that rudderless boat? Let it be one of our first purposes to discover. With the first glimpse we obtain of it, the dawn of our success shall begin.

This boat shall guide us, with a rapidity which will surprise even ourselves, to him who employed it in the midnight of the fatal Sabbath. Corroboration will rise upon corroboration, and the murderer will be traced."

[For reasons which we shall not specify, but which to many readers will appear obvious, we have taken the liberty of here omitting, from the MSS. placed in our hands, such portion as details the *following up* of the apparently slight clew obtained by Dupin. We feel it advisable only to state, in brief, that the result desired was brought to pass; [**that an individual assassin was convicted, upon his own confession, of the murder of Marie Roget,**] and that the Prefect fulfilled punctually, although with reluctance, the terms of his compact with the Chevalier. Mr. Poe's article concludes with the following words—*Eds.**]

It will be understood that I speak of coincidences *and no more*. What I have said above upon this topic must suffice. In my own heart there dwells no faith in præter-nature. That Nature and its God are two, no man who thinks, will deny. That the latter, creating the former, can, at will, control or modify it, is also unquestionable. I say "at will;" for the question is of will, and not, as the insanity of logic has assumed, of power. It is not that the Deity *cannot* modify his laws, but that we insult him in imagining a possible necessity for modification. In their origin these laws were fashioned to embrace *all* contingencies which *could* lie in the Future. With God all is *Now*.

I repeat, then, that I speak of these things only as of coincidences. And farther: in what I relate it will be seen that between the fate of the unhappy Mary Cecilia Rogers, so far as that fate is known, and the fate of one Marie Rogêt up to a certain epoch in her history, there has existed a parallel in the contemplation of whose wonderful exactitude the reason becomes embarrassed. I say all this will be seen. But let it not for a moment be supposed that, in proceeding with the sad narrative of Marie from the epoch just mentioned, and in tracing to its *dénouement* the mystery which enshrouded her, it is my covert design to hint at an extension of the parallel, or even to suggest that the measures adopted in Paris for the discovery of the

---

*Of the Magazine in which the article was originally published. [Not true; see Note 9, Chapter 3—J. W.]

assassin of a grisette, or measures founded in any similar
ratiocination, would produce any similar result.

For, in respect to the latter branch of the supposition, it should
be considered that the most trifling variation in the facts of the two
cases might give rise to the most important miscalculations, by
diverting thoroughly the two courses of events; very much as, in
arithmetic, an error which, in its own individuality, may be
inappreciable, produces, at length, by dint of multiplication at all
points of the process, a result enormously at variance with truth.
And, in regard to the former branch, we must not fail to hold in
view that the very Calculus of Probabilities to which I have
referred, forbids all idea of the extension of the parallel:—forbids it
with a positiveness strong and decided just in proportion as this
parallel has already been long-drawn and exact. This is one of those
anomalous propositions which, seemingly appealing to thought
altogether apart from the mathematical, is yet one which only the
mathematician can fully entertain. Nothing, for example, is more
difficult than to convince the merely general reader that the fact of
sixes having been thrown twice in succession by a player at dice, is
sufficient cause for betting the largest odds that sixes will not be
thrown in the third attempt. A suggestion to this effect is usually
rejected by the intellect at once. It does not appear that the two
throws which have been completed, and which lie now absolutely in
the Past, can have influence upon the throw which exists only in the
Future. The chance for throwing sixes seems to be precisely as it was
at any ordinary time—that is to say, subject only to the influence of
the various other throws which may be made by the dice. And this is
a reflection which appears so exceedingly obvious that attempts to
controvert it are received more frequently with a derisive smile than
with anything like respectful attention. The error here involved—a
gross error redolent of mischief—I cannot pretend to expose within
the limits assigned me at present; and with the philosophical it
needs no exposure. It may be sufficient here to say that it forms one
of an infinite series of mistakes which arise in the path of Reason
through her propensity for seeking truth *in detail*.

Selected Bibliography

The items included here all bear specifically on the Mary Rogers case and The Mystery of Marie Roget. *Poe biographies which treat the subject, as well as the various writings of collateral interest, are identified in the Notes.*

Byrnes, Thomas, *Professional Criminals of America.* New York, 1886, pp. 334-47.

Clemens, Will, "The Tragedy of Mary Rogers." *Era Magazine,* XIV (1904), 450-63.

Costello, R., "Poe and Mary Rogers." *Evening Post* (New York), January 10, 1920, Sec. III, p. 11, col. 4.

Croffut, W. A., "Who Murdered Mary Rogers?" *Free Press* (Detroit), June 13, 1885.

Crouse, R., *Murder Won't Out.* Garden City, New York, 1932, pp. 52-74.

Davis, Andrew J., *Tales of a Physician.* New York, 1869, pp. 192-200.

Duke, T. S., *Celebrated Criminal Cases of America.* San Francisco, 1910, pp. 577-82.

Ingraham, J. H., *The Beautiful Cigar Girl.* New York, 1844. A novel.

Lane, W. D., "The Mystery of Mary Rogers." *Collier's,* March 8, 1930, pp. 19, 50, 52.

Levins, Peter, "Rogers Mystery Formed Basis for Poe Short Story." *Sunday News* (New York), September 21, 1941, pp. 52-53, 55.

Pearce, Charles E., *Unsolved Murder Mysteries.* London, 1924, pp. 225-45.

Pearson, Edmund, *Instigation of the Devil.* New York, 1930, pp. 177-85; same in *Vanity Fair,* July 1929, pp. 59, 110.

Poe, Edgar Allan, "The Mystery of Marie Roget." *The Ladies' Companion* (New York), XVII (November, December, 1842), 15-20, 93-99; (February 1843), 162-67. Revised and reprinted in *Tales,* New York, 1845.

Sun (New York), "The Ghost of Mary Rogers," October 16, 1885.

Tribune (New York), "The Murder of Mary Rogers, a Mystery That Was Never Solved—How Poe preserved it in a story," October 29, 1885.

Trumble, A., *Great Crimes and Criminals of America.* New York, 1881, pp. 7-10; same in *National Police Gazette,* May 1881.

Van Every, Edward, *Sins of New York.* New York, 1930, pp. 95-104.

Wallace, Irving, *The Fabulous Originals.* New York, 1955, pp. 172-215.

Walling, G. W., *Recollections of a New York Police Chief.* New York, 1887, pp. 26-29.

Wimsatt, William K., "Poe and the Mystery of Mary Rogers." *Publications of the Modern Language Association,* LVI (March 1941), 230-48.

——, "Mary Rogers, John Anderson, and Others." *American Literature,* XXI (January 1950), 482-84.

Worthen, Samuel, "A Strange Aftermath of the Mystery of Marie Roget." *Proceedings of the New Jersey Historical Society,* LX (April 1942), 116-23.

——, "Poe and the Beautiful Cigar Girl," *American Literature,* XX (November 1948), 305-12.

Index

The typeface used in this book is Baskerville. The text was composed by Linasec II computerized punched-tape and Linotype, using quad left programming to produce a hyphenless ragged right margin. The book was printed on a Crabtree Perfecting Litho Press, on 70# Mohawk Superfine Softwhite paper. The endpapers are Mohawk Cortlea Terracotta and the book is bound in Bancroft Kennett. It was designed by Norton Schwartzott and manufactured by Wm J Keller Inc., Buffalo, New York.